Surfanthood

Surfanthood

Learning to Serve by Learning to Surf

Mark Read

RESOURCE *Publications* • Eugene, Oregon

SURFANTHOOD
Learning to Serve by Learning to Surf

Copyright © 2021 Mark Read. All rights reserved. Except for brief quotations in critical publications or reviews, no part of this book may be reproduced in any manner without prior written permission from the publisher. Write: Permissions, Wipf and Stock Publishers, 199 W. 8th Ave., Suite 3, Eugene, OR 97401.

Resource Publications
An Imprint of Wipf and Stock Publishers
199 W. 8th Ave., Suite 3
Eugene, OR 97401

www.wipfandstock.com

PAPERBACK ISBN: 978-1-6667-1583-5
HARDCOVER ISBN: 978-1-6667-1584-2
EBOOK ISBN: 978-1-6667-1585-9

JULY 26, 2021

Dedicated to Sophie,

With thanks to Joe, Luke and Pamela for some helpful pointers and Noah and Roam for being with me as I wrote

Contents

Preface | vii

Introduction | 1

Getting in the Water
  Why Are You Getting in the Water? | 21
  Shortboard? Longboard? Goofy or Regular Foot? | 24
  Busy or Dedicated | 28
  Equipment Issues | 32
  We Go Barefoot | 36
  Waxing the Board | 38
  Find your Spot | 43

Paddling Out
  Paddle Through | 49
  Paddle Beyond | 55
  Paddle out and Wait | 61

You in the Water
  It's not about You | 67
  It's not about Standing up | 69
  Knee Deep in the Surf | 75

IN TOO DEEP | 82
NOT EVERY WAVE | 87
BREAKING BOARDS | 91
SPIN CYCLED | 96
GETTING BACK IN | 101
PATIENCE | 106
GOOD HONEST RIDES | 111
DISCIPLINE & PRACTICE | 115
ENERGY | 119
CURRENTS & RIPS | 124
ENJOYMENT | 130
FINISHING A RIDE | 132
FINISHING YOUR SESSION | 136

Others in the Water
"THAT'S MY WAVE" & CUTTING IN | 143
SUPs & BODYBOARDS | 148

CONCLUSION | 151

Bibliography | 155

Preface

It is important at the outset for me to make something clear about myself: I am no expert — neither in surfing, nor in ministry. There those who train ministers, who speak at conferences and who write books — I am not one of them. I have learned a great deal from them and am deeply grateful to them. But if I am honest, it is infrequently that I can see my experiences in theirs. My hope is that you may resonate with what you read here; that this will be a place to find and recognise your own experiences and that I may offer language to them or gift you some means of understanding them.

Over the past 8 years I have been inspired by many stories of hope; events and people that have been personal to me, those that have been reported to me from friends and those I have read or heard about within various Christian media. And within the stories I found most compelling I began to see some patterns or repeated aspects that I have come to recognise as servanthood.

These inspiring stories include figures such as Mother Teresa or Paulo Freire; projects (for want of a much better word) such as Homeboy Industries or The Simple Way, writers such as Samuel Wells and Richard Rohr, scholars such as Walter Brueggemann and Tom Wright, activists such as Alastair McIntosh and Martin Newell. Within their stories, I have come to see a vision of the church that is beautiful and compelling but sadly unfamiliar to me as I embarked on my journey into ministry.

Preface

These stories have continued to make me profoundly hopeful about the future of the church, now more than ever in fact. But this hope comes from hearing, engaging with and participating in the intense labour of criticism that precedes every revolution[1]. I am hopeful not because the evidence particularly points towards a better future but because these stories are creating new possibilities, opening, and stretching the imagination of the church.

I am saddened that colleagues and partners-in-crime have left ministry in the years I have served. The rate of drop out, burn out or fade out is troubling. Serving God is life giving, beautiful and exciting. It is joy itself. And yet there have been moments of significant frustration and grief in just my short ministry. And I have met others in ministry who have been deeply embittered, resentful and in pain. Because we are not doing it right. The shape of what we are doing is not right. The solid, heavy, and large preconceptions about ministry obscure a clear and simple message in Jesus' teaching; that we are to be servants.

I write this after 8 years of full-time ministry, preceded by 4 part-time. I write it now before I forget my experiences. I write it as the transformation of our reality takes another lurching step onward during the COVID-19 pandemic. I write it now because I cannot go surfing, and so the time I would dedicate to that has been dedicated to finally writing down the insights I have gained about serving from the experiences I have had surfing.

These ideas are directed to anyone who has heard the call to any ministry; full-time or part time, voluntary or paid, within a church setting or ministering in other places such as schools, hospitals, local communities etc. It is directed towards those who have recently begun, towards those who are in the midst and towards those who are close to leaving. But I write it so that leaders and decision makers in our denominations, movements and organisations may listen in as well. So that perhaps together we can alter the shape of what we are doing to more adequately reflect what Jesus asks of us.

---

1. Gramsci, *Selections from the Prison Notebooks*, 12.

Introduction

FOR ME THERE HAS ALWAYS been a deep connection between my experience of God and my experience of nature. Even from within a church that starkly overlooked this, discovering God in nature was what fed my faith for many of my early years. When I first began full-time ministry I was in the fortunate position to be close to one of the more beautiful surfing beaches in Britain. Surfing became the centre of my rhythm of spiritual disciplines — offering me silence, solitude, contemplation, repetitive prayer. Each Monday morning I scheduled a "board meeting" in my diary. Parallels quickly began to emerge between what I experienced in the water and what I was experiencing in my ministry. A simple but profound analogy presented itself that has remained with me and developed since. Almost every time I enter the water I am taken into a new insight within the analogy which has provided the content for this book.

The analogy goes like this:
The waves are God's activity in the world.
The surfer is us.
The board is our activity/ministry/service.
This analogy has made increasing sense to me.

The sea is an awesome and generous reality for surfers, offering so much peace and joy whilst simultaneously ferocious and powerful. It is dynamic, generative, constant but not consistent, beautiful but unknowable.

Boards are personal to a surfer; almost no two boards are the same and the link between surfer and surfboard becomes a deep one. Like our boards, activities become personal to us; they feel like part of us. In ways they describe and define who we are.

At best our activities, and boards, join with God's activity, the waves, to create something joyful, wondrous, and exciting. We submit to the wave and experience something beautiful. At worst we can wrestle and struggle becoming increasingly tired, frustrated and pained by what is happening until eventually the inevitable occurs; we get really hurt or we get out.

This simple analogy will flow through the book — waves, surfer, surfboard — paralleling God, us, and ministry in a journey of learning a new way of being.

Because we need to learn a new way.

The old ways are done. Most of the activity of those in ministry is orientated around a paradigm that has been steadily slipping away for decades. The skills of congregational maintenance and leadership will not be needed by many in the future as slowly our entanglements with the empire are severed and the last remnants and recapitulations of Christendom fall away. We are not ready for the reality before us. Few can imagine Christian ministry beyond what they have known and seen. Many will say we were better off before, at least we had shelter and food to eat[1]. But we cannot go back. It is going to be difficult to learn — just like learning to surf.

Whilst I have been encouraged by so many examples of radical faith, extreme love, and profound hopefulness these seem inaccessible to those of us within institutional churches. Do we just leave? Many have, and perhaps this is the way forward. But we must be people who believe in redemption surely. Jesus body was resurrected, and so must the pattern be that the Church dies to itself to find new life?

I should expand this just a little further. It is well-acknowledged that we are in the midst of one of those periods in history when everything is shaken up. It has been described in many ways,

---

1. Exodus 16:3

Introduction

but I think my favourite is the "rummage sale"[2] — everything is up for critique, renegotiation, and rejection. For some time now, within the Western church, the priority has been on particular models and paradigms of leadership that seem heavily influenced by the corporate and commercial world. There have been large global conferences dedicated to it, plenty of books, there are speakers, training schools, courses — a whole industry has been growing to peddle Christian Leadership. This hermeneutic has been applied to Scripture and has widely been accepted. Leadership has saturated our imagination, permeated our minds so fully that it is the default of most. Yet it seems to relegate a key message of Jesus; that the Son of Man came to serve, that the greatest is the one who serves[3]; that it is in servanthood we must find our pattern for living.

Within this rummage sale it can be easy to appear dismissive or overly critical of what has come before: the analogy bears out as we can all imagine a treasured family heirloom being sold for pennies if not properly valued by the seller. However, someone must have the courage to put it on the table in the first place: To inspect it and appraise it. It is good for us to read the edifying of the academic or the comfort or challenge of the pastoral; but there are rarely books that ask us to listen to the disquieting voice of the prophetic: Voices that force us to put things on the table and really scrutinise what they mean to us. And, to depart from the analogy, imagine what could be instead.

No change comes from a just a single voice. There is always a plurality of voices that shape new things and I do not anticipate what I am outlining here to form a new orthodoxy or a new paradigm. Instead, I am hoping to add the voices that are naming what has been with increasing accuracy and nuance and who can see something new coming that they are beginning to describe. I suspect that those who have thrived in what has been will be uncomfortable; those who have enjoyed the congregational focus of the passing paradigm will feel deeply uneasy about welcoming a

2. Tickle, *The Great Emergence*, 8
3. Luke 22:24–30

new one. But we must allow ourselves to be disturbed; to treasure the disquieting so that we may re-find peace. That seems to me one of the important roles of the Psalms[4]. And it is ok if you are unpersuaded at the end; it is not my intention to recruit, merely to offer some thoughts.

Using Luke's gospel as a guide, we will look at what servanthood may mean in our context; reflecting on the process of learning to surf/serve to help us understand experiences and imagine how servanthood can inform and shape us.

Why Luke's gospel?

Before answering this I must first acknowledge that I am reading Luke, within this book, in a way that draws out that which I believe is there. I read it in a way as to interpret the actions and dialogue within the Gospel, as well as Luke's sophisticated constructions of the Gospel, in the light — or through the lens — of Surfanthood; it is the hermeneutic in play here. At points this may seem to stretch or manipulate Scripture to some readers. However, it is important to note that we all bring a hermeneutic to Scripture, we all read it through a particular lens. We do well to acknowledge and explore our lens, even deconstructing it entirely to assess its validity. But we must be very wary of those who claim that they "just read the Bible"; those who are unaware, or even in denial, that they bring much cultural, social, philosophical, political, and emotional material to bear when they are reading and interpreting Scripture. At best they can be poor conversation partners, at worst they can be quite dangerous people.

The Gospel of Luke is written to a broader audience than the other synoptic gospels. Whilst addressed to Theophilus, who is probably a fictive character, Luke writes generally to those members of the Way, Theophilus meaning "Lover of God", who were spread over eastern Asia and southern Europe by the time of Luke's composition. These small groups were being systematically

---

4. W Brueggemann's work on the Psalms of orientation, disorientation and reorientation has been helpful here.

Introduction

uprooted during the period Luke writes. The Pharisees, now the default leaders of the Jewish people after the destruction of the Temple, were tightening the boundaries of their tribe. Those Jews who believed the Messiah was still to come were the faithful and could remain, but this strange new sect of Jews who were including Gentiles and declaring the Messiah had come in the person of Jesus had to go. They were a liability and threat to the whole community.

So Luke's audience suddenly found themselves on the outside of the community; viewed with suspicion and distain whilst still they were seeking to be faithful to Jesus' teaching and develop in their vocation as his followers. I need not labour this point but there are many who will feel a strong resonance with this feeling today: Those who have followed Jesus outside of their tribe, beyond the orthodoxies of their kin and found themselves viewed with similar suspicion and even, perhaps, distain. Luke writes to make those early followers, and those who share that experience today, aware that they are included in something new and that there is a way Jesus set out by which they can find peace with what has passed and joy in what is to come.

Collectively the Gospels address four key questions about being human. Matthew's gospel equips the reader to face change: Written primarily to a Jewish audience Matthew is littered with overt references to Scripture and works hard to bridge the gap between traditional Israelite faith and the belief that Israel's story had reached its fulfilment in Jesus. Mark's gospel supports the reader as they endure suffering: Written after the destruction of the Temple and to followers of Jesus facing persecution within Roman contexts Mark dedicates almost half of his swift and concise Gospel to the Passion narrative. John's gospel opens the reader to experience joy: Written last and very differently to the other Gospels John's use of feasts, gardens, poetry, and symbolism constructs a beautiful gospel entreating its reader to rest in joy and peace. And Luke's equips the reader to mature through service[5].

---

5. Thankful to Alexandra Shaia's work for this

Surfanthood

Often, when beginning any Christian ministry, we are directed straight to Paul and his letters, or to Moses and his leadership. Sadly, we have coloured Paul's letters so heavily with imposed meanings and shallow understandings of prooftexts we have extracted that we can only hear his voice pertain to the church we have experienced: One shaped by recent Western models of leadership and economic practices. It would be too larger task to restore Paul within this book and there are those who have done that work already[6] if we would heed them. Nonetheless, we turn to Luke, who sees beyond the destroyed temple and painful sectarianism, which alone may help us in our current climate. He sees a continuation of God's self-involving promises[7] and points to servanthood as the means by which we are intended to live. After all, Adam and Eve were created to tend and nurture and serve in God's creation and this remains true for humanity. Luke's gospel offers a starting point for ministry centred on service and servanthood.

You will notice at the end of each section a practice. I probably do not need to say but these are spiritual disciplines I have found helpful that relate to what I am describing. The most helpful book I have got on my shelf is Adele Calhoun's 'Spiritual Disciplines Handbook' — a comprehensive, practical, and accessible guide to almost every discipline.

What do I mean by servanthood?

Before continuing it is necessary to establish a clear idea of what I mean specifically by servanthood. It is a *Christianese*[8] word; a slippery term that can be used in all sorts of ways. In this section I will give a quick introduction to five principles of servanthood that I think are helpful. Before I begin though, I must give a warning about the use of language: Language is a difficult thing at the best of times, even more challenging when in the hands of a clumsy

---

6. N T Wright's work on Paul

7. Hays *Echoes of Scripture in the Gospels* 192

8. A language uniquely spoken by Christians that whilst, at times, using recognisable words can be entirely unfamiliar.

Introduction

and imprecise writer. The words I am using are being re-purposed for the ends of this book; they are not being used as they normally are but the precise language for what I am trying to communicate simply does not exist in a concise enough form. So I would ask you to suspend your conceptions of these five terms as I try to outline what I am using them to describe. This will require negotiation between us as we are defining a slippery term with misshapen language.

1. Servanthood is *non-professional*
2. Servanthood is *non-commercial*
3. Servanthood is *non-prescriptive*
4. Servanthood is *non-evangelical*
5. Servanthood is *non-authoritative*.

In many ways, and throughout the rest of the book, servanthood is about resistance and contradiction which is why each principle is framed as being *non-* something. Not *anti*, as this would just mean behaving in the opposite or being in conflict with, but *non*; entailing a need to open a wider scope of alternatives. Servanthood is about resisting the assumptions that much of the church has uncritically accepted and contradicting the principles and practices of the Empire that pervade our culture and too often mark our churches.

Frustratingly Empire is never easily pointed out. It rarely operates overtly and infrequently offers much evidence of itself. Yet, there it lurks; limiting our imaginations so that we cannot conceive of the alternatives. Nonetheless, by the sensitive it is known and recognised; rarely through evidence and indication but through intuition and feeling — two things greatly undervalued in our ways of knowing. There are engrained assumptions about how we should operate as people and as organisations that saturate our imaginations that come to us from Empire: They influence the postures we adopt, the attitudes and characteristics we demonstrate, the deportment with which we carry ourselves. These assumptions are drawn from our culture, yet they are so ubiquitous that we hardly notice them. They have quietly and surreptitiously determined so much and yet we rarely name them. For us to notice them requires a similar process as it would for a fish to comment on how wet water is; the fish's reality is so entirely determined by the water it would be strange if she even noticed it. Yet, notice them we must.

It would be fascinating, but too lengthy, to explore the history of these assumptions and their origins so I trust that we can accept them for now. Some of these assumptions that I have observed most frequently are the new needs[9] of professionalism, commercialism, prescription, evangelism, and authority.

I am aware of a risk in talking about five principles and using servanthood in such a specific manner; that the ideas proposed in this book could be seen as just another solution offered for the church: A new thing to do, a new label to adopt or a new franchise to appropriate. This is certainly not the intention. I have read those "How to. . . " books and found them unsatisfying. Similarly, there are those books that focus their entire energy on closing-down and lampooning things they do not like. But laptops are bad tools for grinding axes. Instead, this is about who you are and how you operate. The book will critique and interrogate some realities, but I will seek to open alternatives more than just close down what already is.

The five principles will be fleshed out in much greater detail throughout the subsequent chapters but to commence a summary concept would be helpful. And for those who just want a quick idea of what this book is about the remainder of this section may suffice. The principles do not neatly divide into five independent concepts — there is much cross-over and recapitulation as ideas are explored from differing angles and perspectives. They are interdependent and inform one another.

First, to help us as we begin, let us consider the encounter between Jesus and the rich and important man.

---

9. Marx *The German Ideology* 21

Introduction

Luke 18: 18–30

A Rich and Important Man

¹⁸ An important man asked Jesus, "Good Teacher, what must I do to have eternal life?"
¹⁹ Jesus said, "Why do you call me good? Only God is good. ²⁰ You know the commandments: 'Be faithful in marriage. Do not murder. Do not steal. Do not tell lies about others. Respect your father and mother.'"
²¹ He told Jesus, "I have obeyed all these commandments since I was a young man."
²² When Jesus heard this, he said, "There is one thing you still need to do. Go and sell everything you own! Give the money to the poor, and you will have riches in heaven. Then come and be my follower." ²³ When the man heard this, he was sad, because he was very rich.
²⁴ Jesus saw how sad the man was. So he said, "It's terribly hard for rich people to get into God's kingdom! ²⁵ In fact, it's easier for a camel to go through the eye of a needle than for a rich person to get into God's kingdom."
²⁶ When the crowd heard this, they asked, "How can anyone ever be saved?"
²⁷ Jesus replied, "There are some things that people cannot do, but God can do anything."
²⁸ Peter said, "Remember, we left everything to be your followers!"
²⁹ Jesus answered, "You can be sure that anyone who gives up home or wife or brothers or family or children because of God's kingdom ³⁰ will be given much more in this life. And in the future world they will have eternal life."

Servanthood is *non-professional*.

The rich and important man would have lent credibility, position and significance to the movement gathering around Jesus, and Jesus' followers recognised this. He represented a new demographic that Jesus was reaching, bringing a wealth of new opportunity; he was a gatekeeper within the community of the affluent and influential. He could offer financial resource; he could offer a network of others like himself and he could describe how to reach further with Jesus' message. His importance would gain them respect as he was a notable figure perhaps well-known in the area, perhaps a celebrity of sorts. The desire to enlist him was obviously great which is why his dismissal provokes such a response from the disciples. With his help they could smarten themselves up a bit, work on their branding and key message. He seems like a gift to this squabbling rabble — he has kept the commands, presumably knows his Scripture. Surely Jesus will welcome him, perhaps even reshuffle the cabinet to give him an appropriate position.

The dynamic of *professionalism* has been unhelpful in ministry. We are seen as being the expert leader, employed or engaged to solve the issues and crises of a church. Professionalism invariably begets paternalism and those you minister to quickly become positioned as beneficiaries of your professional expertise. This has, for so long, been the posture of the church and is well entrenched and reinforced by our systems and habits, language, and practices. For example, there are tasks only a priest may perform, decisions that rest with the leader, roles that can only be filled by the minister. Similarly, often the adults within a church leave all the engagement with young people to the youth worker or work with homelessness to employed experts. We have structured ourselves around autocracy and hierarchy and neglected the priesthood of all believers. We have clung to corporate models of leadership and neglected what we know from the Trinity.

This has yielded some horrible results. Some have sunk under the weight of expectation; pioneers tasked with resurrecting sunken churches, priests responsible for altering the trajectory of large and entrenched churches, youth workers expected to fill congregations with polite, affable young people. Others have relished the position and power that the hierarchy has afforded them and created an empire for themselves where they alone are Caesar.

Introduction

In beautiful contrast to this, a servant may be one beggar telling another beggar where to find bread[10]. We may come as a fellow to participate in fellowship. In that way we discover the riches, gifts, and assets in front of us rather than constantly looking behind, to head offices, diocese etc for resources. Instead of asking "what do I bring to this?" which feeds the ego, we may ask "what have I found here?"

Servanthood is *non-commercial*.

The Rich and Important man leads with a loaded question. "What must I do to inherit eternal life?" I will not waste time unpacking how this is not a question about going to heaven — this has been more than adequately explained elsewhere. It is not the first time Jesus is asked this question in Luke's gospel. The previous occasion a teacher of the law asks and this elicits the parable of the Good Samaritan. Here, Jesus perceives different motivations. This is about commodification. The man has wealth, power, position, and piety, yet is unsatisfied. He wants something else. He is hoping Jesus will fulfil his desire. Instead, Jesus invites him to divest himself of what he has already gained and follow him. This makes no sense to the man. Why give up what is already earned and secured? He is looking to ice his cake, not give it away. He is hoping to find a sense of completion rather than the fulfilment he is ultimately offered. Furthermore, why would he give up that which should make him so appealing to Jesus as a potential follower? Looking at the rest of Jesus' young and unimpressive disciples the man may have assumed Jesus would be lucky to have him.

Elements of transaction of investment are detrimental to authentic ministry. In the biopic of the track cyclist Graeme Obree, The Flying Scotsman, Obree struggles with mental health and is befriended by Douglas Baxter, a minister. After some time Obree admits his apprehension that Baxter was just "after his soul". When we undertake service to another with an ulterior motive it is easily

10. D T Niles perhaps

sniffed out and undermines that which we are doing. Service is done as its own thing, for its own intrinsic beauty and integrity. Yet, too often, activity is determined by what will be beneficial to the church. It can be easy to adopt a mind-set that seeks gains in profit or profile, power, or position.

Commercialism can be a repeated pattern in which we often fail to respond as Jesus does: a project we start gains momentum and suddenly there are professional agencies involved, a programme we undertake is successful and funders appear to sponsor it, a group we meet with grows in membership and some exciting, gifted, and capable people arrive to join in. Before we know it, we are swept into *commercialism*. And once we are, we notice that the project stops feeling as life-giving, the programme becomes unwieldy, ceases to serve those it was created for and feels like an advertising campaign for the funders and the original members of the group we were meeting with stop coming as they do not feel as comfortable anymore. Yet, so frequently we fail to resist the offer of the rich and important man as his temptations are too great for us.

Service is offered not to secure the satisfaction of the servant, but of the one who is served. There are frequent times when a minor celebrity or local dignitary rolls up their sleeves for a quick photo-shoot of them do-gooding. Similarly, many capable, gifted, and well-meaning people arrive to help out with things from time to time. These probably should not be met with hostility but we must be aware of the motivation of *commercialism* that is behind them; they are rounding out their collections, completing a set or raising a profile. More personally, how often do we commercialise our own activity; dwelling on the great gifts and resources we can offer and growing frustrated when those around us do not avail themselves of the opportunity we represent.

Servanthood is *non-prescriptive.*

We must make some assumptions here that are not demonstrably clear within Luke's story of the rich and important man. We know he was an important man, so can assume he was successful

Introduction

in whatever it was that he did. How easy would he have found it to submit to Jesus' teachings? Obviously not particularly easy as he could not follow Jesus' first command to him. But suppose Jesus had enlisted him anyway. How would he have responded to Jesus' embarrassing and scruffy procession into Jerusalem on Palm Sunday? How would he have reacted to Jesus' mistreatment and abuse of the merchants in the Temple? Or to his incendiary answer about paying taxes, or his astounding claim about the Temple being destroyed, or his allowing himself to be crucified as just another insurrectionist? None of these actions made sense and no-one would prescribe them if trying to accomplish the liberation of God's people and the establishment of a new kingdom. Anyone who had been successful in anything knew you needed to keep the powerful on side; that you needed to behave efficiently and effectively, that you needed to go about things in a completely different way to how Jesus was behaving. I suspect, like Judas, this rich and important man would ultimately have been too dissatisfied with how Jesus behaved.

Servants respond to the needs that present themselves rather than undertaking activity prescribed from elsewhere. There is not one thing you should be doing and there is not one way to do it. Responding to needs seems to provoke fear amongst many churches around merely "needs meeting" — an accusation often levelled at acts of service that seemingly gain nothing for our congregation. However true service is necessarily reactionary: It entails activity instigated by someone else.

Perhaps Jesus perceives how difficult it is for the successful to lay down the means of their success; their leadership, decision making, organising, strategizing; their determination of activity and behaviour. How difficult it is to relinquish these tools of success. And how difficult it is not to try and employ them in the service of the church. And yet, Jesus sends the man away to relinquish them so that he may enter the Kingdom; where he must yield to Jesus Lordship, where he must be obedient to the will of God, where he must respond to the Spirit's activity and where he must become a servant to others.

However, servanthood does not mean we must be simplistic; servants can respond with complex, nuanced, and considered activity and they can be highly skilled individuals — but they act in response to others. When servants decide their own activity, they set out on a road to idolatry. We find a helpful parable illustrating just this in Luke 20: 9–15. In this way, servanthood is *non-prescriptive*: you do not offer solutions, programmes, strategies but instead allow activity to be initiated and determined outside of yourself.

Servanthood is *non-evangelical*.

Even on a surface reading, Luke's account demonstrates something at odds with our own assumptions about what church must, and must not, do. Jesus sends the man away. He, ultimately, does not join. This seems entirely contradictory to what we have learned about evangelism — where everyone is invited to join. And if we peer beneath the surface there is more to substantiate how counter-intuitive Jesus' reaction is for us. Enlisting the man would not have just meant welcoming one convert; he brought with him the means to reach a much larger audience. Presumably, he had a whole household of servants, employees, and dependants who he could convert at his will. And think of all the additional towns and cities that could be visited with the money he could provide. Think of all the palaces of power and places of position his profile could enable access to. He was an evangelist's gift and yet Jesus turns him away.

This word has become so heavily burdened with notions of Imperialism and paternalism. Evangelism has become less about sharing good news and more about winning converts to a tribe. If Jesus' intention were to amass as greater crowd as possible why would he ask people to return home, or deny permission for them to follow him? Evangelism seems predicated on the logic that you conscript as many people as possible to your tribe. By means of intellectual persuasion or emotional cajoling you convince them of your argument and then begin a process of "discipleship" which

Introduction

fills them with your orthodoxy and orthopraxy so they can, in turn, go forth and begin conscripting more people to your tribe.

This is heavily prescriptive, as you tell others exactly what they need to do and believe. It is highly commercial as you are commodifying what you are offering; brokering a transaction and upscaling your operations as quickly as possible [I remember being amused by a diagram in a lecture about "Cell Church" — a church fad from the early 2000s — which looked exactly like a pyramid scheme]. And evangelicalism thrives on professionalism; those with skills, strategy, and resources at their disposal can amass large crowds fairly quickly. Those who have succinct and intelligent branding and successful operational models can quickly replicate what they are doing elsewhere to expand their tribe.

Evangelism, mission, and pioneering are words encumbered with imprecise and unhelpful ideas. They seem distinctly orientated around the Church and its advantage: Undertaking evangelism to swell our crowds, engaging in mission to establish our position in the world and pioneering to discover untapped resources and territories to expand into. Underneath all that unappealing and ugly commercialism lurks the far more dangerous motivation; the belief that one tribe has it right and can prescribe what others need to know and do. Herein lies the arrogance of evangelicalism; confident it has so thoroughly understood God — the infinite and incomprehensible — that it is willing to package Him up and sell Him to others.

It seems truer to Jesus' teaching for us to learn the depths of service than to wrestle with evangelicalism, mission and pioneering. Evangelicalism seems to move in the opposite direction to that most foundational piece of Biblical theology; the incarnation, where God became fully human. He became like us rather than making us like him. There is a much deeper truth about us being made in His likeness and image within this but just to look at the direction of travel is important. We seek to make others like us in converting them, whereas he sought to be like us in the incarnation. Perhaps we could discover God in others rather than trying to prescribe God to them.

Surfanthood

Servanthood is *non-authoritative*.

We return to the text of the rich and important man. He is a man accustomed to making his own decisions. His wealth and position had made him an authority, he was used to giving orders and determining the direction. And so his disobedience of Jesus feels inevitable. He does not go and sell all he has; he does not give the money to the poor and he does not return to follow Jesus. Presumably this is because he could not understand why he needed to divest himself of all that has secured him position and power. He may be interested, even compelled by Jesus but does not obey him. We can suppose this is because Jesus is not interesting or compelling enough, but I do not feel this gets us far. Rather, it is about submission. The rich and important man is not willing to allow Jesus to have authority over him. He may accept partnership with Jesus; perhaps he would be willing to cooperate or work alongside the Messiah, or to give generously donations to this exciting young Rabbi. But to relinquish his authority, to allow himself to be stripped of his position and wealth and adopt a position of submission is beyond what he can do. Jesus goes on to say how it is hard for any rich person to enter the Kingdom because to do so they must become *non-authoritative*.

In our language, particularly the phrases that appear in songs and prayers, we often utter our underlying desire for the church, and for ourselves, to be given positions of authority. I have winced at supplications for God to "raise up his Church" and "give us power". Similarly, I have sat in lectures and seminars where the advice was to find the "gatekeepers" as a priority; find the influencers in a congregation and the stakeholders in a community. Get close to the centres of power and begin to accumulate some authority. It does not resonate with what I see Jesus doing; who heads for the forgotten and the marginalised; who dismisses the powerful and important. He does not seek a position of authority.

In adopting a *non-authoritative* posture servants are not burdened with maintaining orthodoxy or orthopraxis and so are liberated to do as they are asked. Too much time and energy has been

Introduction

spent herding theological cats and trying to impose uniformity of practice within denominations. A cursory glance at church history announces clearly that the more determined we have been to define orthodox belief the more we have fractured and splintered the body of Christ. Servants are afforded the benefit of not worrying about what is believed by another about God. Instead, they are engaged in discovering God as they work with another.

Servants do not make decisions. They practice obedience. In a sobering thought, perhaps Luke's encounter of the rich and important man may be highly prophetic. Perhaps the rich and important man symbolises not just an individual, but the Church. Perhaps it is the Church who is in grief as we cannot relinquish that which gives us authority in order to submit to Jesus and so gain increasing distance from him as we walk in the opposite direction.

As is so often the case, the disciples give language to our feelings. How could Jesus dismiss this man? How could he not take advantage of the gift he offered? If this man is not good enough, qualified enough, desirable enough the how can anyone be saved? And then, with comedic irony, Peter's rebuke of Jesus for dismissing this potential source of wealth and comfort to their movement opens our eyes to what it is that Jesus is looking for. "Remember, we left everything to be your followers". Yes Peter, that's the point. You gave it all up. In turn, we must surely consider giving up our professionalism, commercialism, prescription, evangelicalism, and authority.

Getting in the Water

Why Are You Getting in the Water?

THERE WERE TIMES AS I started surfing that all I was really doing was getting in the water for a swim with my board. I was not really looking for waves, just paddling to-and-fro. These sessions never ended well. I'd get in the way of other surfers, I'd get caught off guard by waves. One time I had been so distracted I did not notice a curious seal just beside me and we both got the fright of our lives as I squawked at him and flopped off the board into the water. Eventually I learned that if I was going in, I needed to be going in to surf. It had to be the intent and motivation to what I was doing.

Luke 5:1-11

Jesus Chooses His First Disciples

> [1] Jesus was standing on the shore of Lake Gennesaret, teaching the people as they crowded around him to hear God's message. [2] Near the shore he saw two boats left there by some fishermen who had gone to wash their nets. [3] Jesus got into the boat that belonged to Simon and asked him to row it out a little way from the shore. Then Jesus sat down in the boat to teach the crowd.
> [4] When Jesus had finished speaking, he told Simon, "Row the boat out into the deep water and let your nets down to catch some fish."

⁵ "Master," Simon answered, "we have worked hard all night long and have not caught a thing. But if you tell me to, I will let the nets down." ⁶ They did it and caught so many fish that their nets began ripping apart. ⁷ Then they signalled for their partners in the other boat to come and help them. The men came, and together they filled the two boats so full that they both began to sink.

⁸ When Simon Peter saw this happen, he knelt down in front of Jesus and said, "Lord, don't come near me! I am a sinner." ⁹ Peter and everyone with him were completely surprised at all the fish they had caught. ¹⁰ His partners James and John, the sons of Zebedee, were surprised too.

Jesus told Simon, "Don't be afraid! From now on you will bring in people instead of fish." ¹¹ The men pulled their boats up on the shore. Then they left everything and went with Jesus.

For a long time this passage posed difficulties for me. I had always felt intensely guilty for not longing to "bring in" lots of people to join congregations I have been part of or even led. It has never been a priority. Initially I attributed it to differences in giftings — "some are teachers, some prophets, some evangelists" — this sort of got me off the hook. But it was deeper than that. It was not just that I was not fussed about rounding up new members myself, I was not really too concerned about anyone doing this sort of thing and could not really understand the intense motivation of some of my colleagues. I would go to ecumenical planning meetings and feel uneasy at the underlying, or even overt, objective of all that was spoken about being church growth. Similarly, I would cringe during seminars, lectures and workshops that described how to implement church growth strategies.

Over time I gained language for my feelings of unease. It was the

1. commercialism of mission: that we needed to brand and market and advertise to attract attention and interest in people joining our tribe and adopting our orthodoxy.

Why Are You Getting in the Water?

2. commodification of salvation: that somehow God had appointed only us to offer people this unique thing that could make them like us if only they would bite.

And I saw the anguish and frustration of my colleagues after another of the many ecumenical efforts yielded an underwhelming result. We didn't pray enough. The PA system wasn't loud enough. The flyers weren't distributed early enough.

Then something clicked about what Jesus, and those he called, understood by what he was saying. Fishermen spent their time on shore sorting their catch — separating the good fish from those they would discard. In Jeremiah 16 YHWH enlists Israel's enemies to haul them in like fish as an enactment of his judgement. Jesus was not calling those first disciples to embark on a *commercial* campaign with him, touring the areas to amass the largest possible following. He was calling them to participate in the judgement of Israel; to call time on the corrupted system that had turned his father's house into "place where robbers hide"[1]. This was a very different vocation to the one I had believed they were being called to. And, if I am honest, far more compelling to me. Not that I wanted to go into the streets and start haranguing people about judgement. But, instead, the call to participate in restoring and redeeming how faith is demonstrated and lived by God's people.

Servanthood is *non-prescriptive*. I had taken the prescribed activity of a church leader, despite it not feeling comfortable, despite it making me uneasy, as read. Uncritically I had assumed that congregational growth was what we were supposed to do.

It is tempting now to advise that we are certain of what we are getting in the water to do. But I need to resist that and remember what I actually learned. Be open to what might be offered, be critical of the prescriptions, expectations and desires you may have and that others might have of you. Get behind them and examine their motivations and origins.

Practice examen.

---

1. Luke 19:46

Shortboard? Longboard? Goofy or Regular Foot?

Before starting to surf we must discover something about ourselves. What sort of surfer are we? It can be problematic because what we need to discover about ourselves can only be done by surfing, but it may be difficult to surf without knowing. It is a paradox but most muddle their way through to discover if they are a longboarder or shortboarder. These are the two key distinctions between surfboards. The two different types of board behave very differently in the water and illicit two distinct styles of surfing. Longboarders enjoy long steady rides; calm, graceful and serene. Shortboarders enjoy energy-filled, exciting, and dynamic rides. The goofy or regular foot refers to some something innate, unchosen, and often unconsidered: the position of a surfer's feet on a board. Regular feet means left foot forward. Goofy means right foot forward.

Consider Paul, Peter, and John's examples in Luke-Acts.

If Paul were a surfer, he would be a shortboarder. Paul appears indefatigable; constantly on the go, pressing on. He is quick, turns sharply and is captivating to watch. I suspect this is why he is so interesting for so many Church leaders who dedicate much time to Paul's writing.

Peter is described by Jesus as the Rock. Whilst within the Gospel he often takes the place of the reader; misunderstanding crucial teachings, behaving at times with poor instincts and inappropriate reactions. Nonetheless, Peter's development to maturity is well chronicled as he becomes a steady and solid leader for the embryonic church. Peter parallels a longboarder wonderfully. He serves the early church as its first elder, already holding together this diverse and disparate group with grace and depth. This must have required poise, balance, and stability — like a longboarder. Whilst there are a few notable twists and turns in his service; the revelation about clean and unclean foods and his rebuke from Paul, he seems to maintain a steady trajectory.

John seems to have remained with Jesus' followers in Jerusalem. Serving as an elder but not journeying like some others. To be an apostle who does not go anywhere may seem to be antithetical. However, it opens our minds that as servants we are sent but may be sent to the community we are already part of. Like a surfer who only surfs their local break John knows the context and community intimately, but we will come back to these ideas in time.

Paul, Peter, and John all served the church in distinctly different ways. We all minister differently. Our style cannot be prescribed to us; often it is innate — a culmination of the gifts and experiences we have. Some surfers appear frantic; full of energy, churning and carving the waves which they constantly pursue and catch. Others are far less frequent in their rides; they appear to move slower with a grace and beauty to what they are doing and remain on a single wave for lengthy periods.

Do you recognise the parallels with yourself and others in ministry you know? Some are constantly starting new things, generating new projects and programmes; getting involved in this and that. They are hard to keep up with and can be both exciting and exhausting to watch. Others seem to find a ministry and so wholly commit to it, gaining deeper and deeper connection to it and appearing so stable, strategic, and measured in their decisions. They are beautiful to watch for a moment but can, in time, appear disinteresting to some wanting a more thrilling experience.

The parallel extends beyond just how we individually surf to the context we find ourselves in. For those with large, established churches, projects, or programmes they have a stability and buoyancy — like a longboard. They have been going for years and are unlikely to stop anytime soon. Like a longboard they will catch a wave and ride it for a long period of time, which can provide a security and enjoyment.

It can also be frustrating. There is little agility. If a change of direction is needed it will need a huge amount of energy. If a wave comes it can be incredibly difficult to reposition for it. At times, the board can feel cumbersome and unwieldy. The large institution that has offered buoyancy and support becomes a frustration and point of challenge with its lack of agility.

In contrast, shortboards are immensely agile. Smaller, often younger, less established churches, projects or programmes can be quick and manoeuvrable. When they see an opportunity to catch a wave they can respond rapidly. When they need a change in direction they can turn on a six-pence/dime. They are not entangled or encumbered with too much protocol or permission gates and so can be reactive. This can be hugely exciting and feel very dynamic.

But there are also drawbacks. They are less buoyant; and so require huge amounts of energy to catch a wave. Surfers must paddle frantically to get up to speed before dropping into a wave. And once they are moving, without the size and stability of a larger board one slight mistake can end the ride.

Ministries do not fall neatly into two categories, nor do ministers, nor do surfers really. This represents a spectrum of experience and approach. The danger in it all is envy. Comparison is the thief of joy[1]. Those feeling the restrictions and sluggishness of being in a large established setting may look with envy at those who can quickly reposition and take on new ideas and activities. They may envy the attention these receive (people on the beach tend to watch the shortboarders for the tricks and excitement of their rides). Conversely those in smaller, less established settings may envy the security and support available to those in larger settings: The ease with which they can catch even the smaller waves because of their size and resources. They can quickly feel exhausted

1. Theodore Roosevelt

Shortboard? Longboard? Goofy or Regular Foot?

at paddling and paddling and getting nowhere and envy those who gracefully float along.

Servants must increasingly seek to know themselves. They must devote time to self-knowing in order to serve well. Their style of service cannot be prescribed to them — it is something innate and unlearned. There are some who may try and prescribe how we should serve/surf but we must resist and discover ourselves.

Practice silence.

Busy or Dedicated

SURFING CAN BE QUITE CONSUMING. The preparation for surfing can also feel fairly involved: Waxing the board, cleaning, and treating wetsuits, exercises and stretches, researching surfing locations, examining tides and waves, finding parking spots, getting the board in or out, or on off, the car etc. At times all this can feel prohibitive. It requires dedication and can, if not balanced, make you busy.

Luke 10: 38–42

Mary and Martha

> [38] The Lord and his disciples were traveling along and came to a village. When they got there, a woman named Martha welcomed him into her home. [39] She had a sister named Mary, who sat down in front of the Lord and was listening to what he said. [40] Martha was worried about all that had to be done. Finally, she went to Jesus and said, "Lord, doesn't it bother you that my sister has left me to do all the work by myself? Tell her to come and help me!"
> [41] The Lord answered, "Martha, Martha! You are worried and upset about so many things, [42] but only one thing is necessary. Mary has chosen what is best, and it will not be taken away from her."

Often this story is used to degrade service or activism: Martha is busy in the kitchen and wants Mary to help but Mary is

Busy or Dedicated

sitting in the presence of Jesus which we come to understand as more important. Most of us will have heard that teaching at some point. Perhaps we have even given it. We have advocated prayer or contemplation as the priority over the business of activism. But perhaps we have misconstrued what is happening here. Perhaps we have imposed our understanding of how households work in the 21st century upon a far more ancient and different culture.

Put simply, I do not believe any more that Martha was washing up. I do not believe she was preparing a meal with an apron on, pots boiling and flour on her face as we can so often imagine. There are some details that we must notice that can deepen our understanding. Firstly, Mary and Martha have a house together and Martha is the one that welcomes Jesus. This is unusual. Were either of Mary or Martha married then it would have been the husband that welcomed Jesus into the home as the leader of the household, such as when they are at the house of Simon the Pharisee, or when Jesus visits Zacchaeus, or the other important Pharisee who is admittedly unnamed but still referred to as the leader of the household. So, Mary and Martha are unmarried; yet do not live in their parents' home. If their parents were alive this is where they would be, and it would be referred to as their father's household.

This was the convention that Luke observes despite being quite powerfully egalitarian at other moments. And so, for Luke to name it as Martha's house is significant. It would be highly unusual for women to own property but not impossible; the most likely prospect is that their parents have died, and no relative has been available to take on the household. So, Martha has done it. We know that there is some wealth to their estate as later in Luke, when their brother Lazarus dies he is placed in a tomb; tombs were highly expensive and so only the wealthy would be able to have one such as Lazarus's. And so, Martha's profile seems to be very different to the kitchen skivvy we may have initially thought of; she is a strong female leader who manages the affairs of a wealthy household; managing staff, organising work, negotiating their business. Martha is pretty unconventional which makes some of what happens a bit ironic.

Getting in the Water

Mary is sitting at Jesus feet. Whilst Martha is busy making security and success for them Mary is being attentive to Jesus; Mary is seeking to be a disciple. It is not that Mary is not serving, it is that she is serving a different end to the one Martha has invested in; one of being a disciple of Jesus. In fact, in many ways Martha has become a slave, rather than the servant we imagine. She is bound to the viability of her household, enslaved by social convention and acceptability. This is why she is so worried about all that had to be done; she is anxious.

Perhaps Martha's outburst is actually her trying to save her sister from embarrassment: A woman could not become a disciple; it was not the convention. Perhaps she is trying to offer Jesus a means to dismiss Mary's desires without having to hurt her feelings; offering him the option to say something like 'Yes Mary, go and help your sister'. This is ironic because Martha must have broken with social convention when she took on the household; and broke with convention daily by managing it. But often those who have made decided steps in a certain direction cannot fathom anyone's choice to move in another. Martha had fought social convention for the security of the household and the respectability this afforded them and now Mary wants to forsake these and bring embarrassment upon herself.

But Jesus recognises Mary's choice. Perhaps the care Martha has for her sister is about more than embarrassment. There were dangers and risks involved with being a disciple, travelling dangerous roads, surviving by the generosity and kindness of strangers. Martha knows this well as she is acting as one of those strangers at the time. Again, Jesus dismisses Martha's offer to reject Mary and gives credence to the choice she is making: A choice to venture into the social unacceptability and into the risk of being a disciple.

There are mixed responses to telling people you surf. I like to think most people think it is an interesting thing to do; but there are certainly some assumptions made. I remember a congregation member remarking to me that before I arrived they had been worried about how much work I would get done as they assumed I would always be in the sea if I lived that close to good surfing.

Their views had been shaped by listening to the beach-boys and watching films that pastiche surfers as "beach-bums" who do little apart from enjoy themselves. Similarly, whenever there is a significant storm in the area I get a message from my Dad warning me not to go surfing because it might be too dangerous. Others have their perceptions shaped by YouTube videos of guys surfing huge waves so that they see surfing as being about thrill-seeking and risk taking. To be a disciple is to take on being socially unacceptable; not to work for security or stability of our households such as Martha, not to recognise social conventions if they are contrary to following Jesus. It is also to take on some risks.

Before we get in the water we must be aware that this is how we may be seen; that we are embarking on something alternate to the mainstream. I am sure that as you have journeyed towards ministry someone has asked you: "Are you sure about doing this?" Are you sure it is what you want to do? Or perhaps people tried to persuade you that ministry is too risky or too consuming. I do not believe we should jump in without thinking but we must be mindful of the voices such as Martha's that would seek to retain us within social acceptability and safety.

Mary's commitment to service goes beyond business to dedication. She is devoting her life to following Jesus despite the costs entailed. We can read this short episode as an encouragement to be still and just listen to Jesus; this is certainly not an unhelpful thing. But the passage has more within it; it is an encouragement to be devoted and fully commit to discipleship and service.

Practice Stewardship.

Equipment Issues

SURFERS CAN BECOME OBSESSIVE ABOUT equipment. The right length fins, at the right angle. The right length board to the inch. The right waxes for the temperature of the sea. Applied in the right pattern. The right shape nose for the board, the right shape tail. The combinations and permutations are endless. Some surfers can invest a huge amount of money and time collecting together and sorting equipment to get the board just right without ever really riding it.

LUKE 9:1–6

Instructions for the Twelve Apostles

> [1] Jesus called together his twelve apostles and gave them complete power over all demons and diseases. [2] Then he sent them to tell about God's kingdom and to heal the sick. [3] He told them, "Don't take anything with you! Don't take a walking stick or a traveling bag or food or money or even a change of clothes. [4] When you are welcomed into a home, stay there until you leave that town. [5] If people won't welcome you, leave the town and shake the dust from your feet as a warning to them."
> [6] The apostles left and went from village to village, telling the good news and healing people everywhere.

Equipment Issues

Jesus sends out his servants with a noticeable lack of usual travelling equipment and there must be a reason. Three specific necessities are denied the apostles: No stick. No money. No spare clothes.

Travelling without a stick would mean that whilst travelling the often-dangerous roads; rocky mountain passes with the risk of encountering thieves or wild animals, the apostles had *no security*. Travelling without any money would mean that when they passed through a place or arrived, they could not buy food and could have *no self-reliance*. Travelling without a spare set of clothes would mean that when they arrived at their final destination they could not get washed and changed into something clean before presenting themselves — but instead would appear in presumably fairly dirty, worn travelling clothes meaning little, or *no dignity* was afforded them. Why would Jesus want his apostles to travel with no security, no self-reliance, and no dignity?

Perhaps today we enjoy some of what Jesus asked his apostles to deny themselves. Ministers are afforded a great level of security: Vicarages and manses. Stipends and allowances. We are unlikely to be fired or made redundant. We are also given everything we need; training, support staff, technical expertise, resources etc. We can be self-reliant. Within our communities we are often well-thought of by virtue of our job; trusted, treated with a level of respect: Asked to take positions in civic ceremonies, asked to preside over events and occasions. We have ceremonial robes and suits, ties, hats, and outfits. We are well-regarded and afforded dignity.

Should we carefully read Jesus' instructions and forego the almost innate security, self-reliance, and dignity of our positions we may notice a shift towards something deeper. Our lack of security may become vulnerability. And so, we can more easily allow ourselves to "be with"[1] those we are amongst. We can let go of needing to be the professional Christian and allow that vulnerability to cultivate honesty and mutuality.

If we forego the ample resources at our disposal, we may begin to notice that our lack of self-reliance becomes a shift towards

---

1. Wells *The Nazareth Manifesto* 12

simplicity. And so, we can allow others to bring what they have, to fill the gaps in what we offer. We can let go of the commercialism of amassing, brokering, and distributing resources from outside our communities and discover what is inside them. In doing this we may move towards being more sustainable as we reduce our dependency on finite resources and discover the infinite generosity that is gifted to us.

If we can relinquish our dignity, although I suspect this may be the toughest for many of us, we may feel a move towards humility. And so, we can be amongst, rather than in front of our communities. We can enjoy and participate instead of enduring and being responsible by taking ourselves out of the middle of things. In doing this we may let go of our self-importance and learn the heart of servanthood.

I wonder how much energy is poured into getting the equipment of our ministries "right". The building projects, the furniture, the computer facilities, the audio-visual set up, the training, the resources, even the people we are amongst become commodified within the commercialism of our endeavours. Those with little can find themselves justifying their frustrations with "I haven't got . . . " or complaining to others that they could "If they had . . . ". We can be like a surfer frustrated at not catching a succession of waves and saying to themselves; if only I had a slightly more buoyant board, then I would be carving and flying down the line. When in wealthy, well-resourced settings energy is spent less on complaining about our deficits and instead we put it into rearranging the equipment. Like a surfer constantly removing and replacing fins and leashes to get just the right effect.

Sadly, we see both of these in the micro and macro. Most denominations in the past decade have undergone huge organisational restructures to maximise their resources. There is nothing wrong with the desire, but the results have, to greater or lesser degrees, made little difference to the ministry that is happening. Tweaks and changes to boards are often imperceptible and the reality is what is probably needed is just more time in the water learning how to use what is there.

Equipment Issues

There also seems to be an unyielding search for the panacea for church issues. It seems there is a belief that if we can find the right "thing" then the pattern of decline will be halted: We have needed youth workers, messy churches, fresh expressions, pioneers, an internet following etc. The list goes on, perhaps because we are unwilling to accept that the decline is an inevitability, and perhaps even desirable as it may remove the security, self-reliance, and dignity to which we cling so tightly despite Jesus' instructions.

This is not to say that youth work, messy church, fresh expressions, or pioneering are not good. But they cannot be tasked to "save" the church. They serve it. But when used as a silver bullet they are unable to bring what they offer; instead, they are loaded with pressure that they cannot bear. I suspect that if we asked those who birthed or undertake these ministries, we would hear them cry out that we not use them in such a way — that we refrain from commodifying them into our commercialisation of mission. Instead, we use them to serve our communities if they are what is needed.

Realistically it is easy to blame things external to ourselves: Our equipment or even the sea itself. But a good surfer can surf on most boards and in most conditions. There are deeper principals guiding their activity and shaping their praxis meaning they can adapt and respond and still enjoy and thrive throughout their session. If we allow our ministry to be determined externally then ministry may feel like trying to wrestle the wrong board to catch the wrong wave and we will find ourselves longing for the idealised situation we have created in our minds: the perfect commercialised system of external inputs and internal rewards. However, if we are freed from the commercialism to explore the alternative; being vulnerable, dependant on others and humble, then we may discover that unwieldy board works brilliantly on the waves if it is used a little differently.

Practice simplicity.

We Go Barefoot

OK, NOT ALWAYS. WHERE I surf the ocean is pretty cold, especially in winter, so often I wear boots. But the principle remains and on the days, I can go barefoot I do; because it is better. When you are barefoot you feel the board more, the connection is better, the grip, the sensitivity. You can adjust and adapt and manoeuvre with more confidence. There is something magical about the feeling of water and wax on bare feet.

Luke 24:27

> [27] And beginning with Moses and all the Prophets, he explained to them what was said in all the Scriptures concerning himself.

Moses was instructed to take off his sandals by the burning bush because it was holy ground. Presumably it had always been holy, but the very obvious indicator of a burning bush awoke Moses to a deeper reality and understanding. But why take off his sandals? Moses shoes were probably made of something else; another creature's skin. Moses had always had identity issues; born a Hebrew, raised a royal Egyptian, now living with the Midians as a shepherd. God cut through all these layers of convoluted identity to call Moses to attention; God asked him to remove that which he used to cover himself so that he might truly know not only God but himself.

The application of this is simple. We must minister in our own skin. We can allow the predispositions of professionalism or prescription to determine who and how we should be. These layers of convoluted identity protect and shield us from knowing who God is and who we are. Not only does it damage us; creating dissonance and dulling our instincts, it rings of inauthenticity to those we are amongst. We may find once these layers are removed our abilities to adapt and manoeuvre heighten. We may discover the magical feeling of wax and water in our ministry.

Practice detachment.

Waxing the Board

Boards need waxing. Boards are made with a smooth resin that, when wet, is pretty slippery. Without a good layer of wax there would be no way of standing on one. So, waxing the board is creating a surface that will shed enough water and create enough texture for the foot to grip. Each surfer will do this slightly differently. Some spend time in their garage carefully setting down a base layer and then building up a top layer with a comb: a careful repetitive process. Others will grab a wax block out the car and quickly scrub some onto the board in the car park before heading into the water.

Luke 11: 1–13

[1] When Jesus had finished praying, one of his disciples said to him, "Lord, teach us to pray, just as John taught his followers to pray."

[2] So Jesus told them, "Pray in this way:

> 'Father, help us
> to honour your name.
> Come and set up
> your kingdom.
> [3] Give us each day
> the bread we need.
> [4] Forgive our debts,

as we forgive everyone
who is in debt to us.
And keep us
from being tempted.'"

This prayer is far more subversive than I had realised when I first began to murmur it along with whatever group of Christians I was with at the time. It seems the huge political and personal notes can be omitted in our recitations leaving just a harmless melody to hum along with. There is much to take notice of and many have given this prayer careful attention. However, there are some points to draw out that serve our purposes here.

"Help us to honour your name" has a strong link to the third of the ten commandments: Do not take the LORD's name in vain. As a child this always perplexed me; in amongst these ten weighty decrees was one about cursing. It just felt a little out of place. However, the Hebrew word translated here as *take* is *nasa'* which more accurately translates as *to carry* or to *lift up;* to bear his name with honour. When the high priest got dressed he would wear a plate with YHWH written upon it — he was literally bearing God's name. This was symbolic to the people of Israel that they had been appointed as his vassal in the world and so must live accordingly, bringing honour to YHWH by living justly, mercifully and with faithfulness to YHWH and one another. They did not work under their own name. In fact, Israel means *YHWH persists*: their name was a testament to YHWH's activity and so the third commandment was about not bearing the Lord's name for no reason; the people had to reflect the character of YHWH. When read in this way the commandment made more sense as a core belief. Similarly, to Israel, servants throughout history would not have been known by individual names; they would be known by the house or name of their master. In bearing God's name servants adopt a humble posture. Not doing their work to bring glory to themselves or advance their standing or advantage. In this way, Jesus' prayer advocates *non-professionalism* by commencing with a reminder of our mandate to serve YHWH's will and purposes.

The true impact of the phrase "set up your kingdom" is trivialised by many of our imaginations. We are quite content with the consumer-capitalism, individualism, and imperialism of our societies. When we utter the words "set up your kingdom" we can mean something incidental; perhaps a veneer of Christianity over what already exists — like his kingdom would be the icing on our adequately-established cake. We fail to fully comprehend. Jesus is teaching this prayer to men from the Galilee: former fishermen, terrorists, and tax collectors. Men who had lived under the oppression of the Roman Empire veiled within the cruelty of the Herodian dynasty. There were very real kingdoms that touched their lives already. To pray that God would come and establish his kingdom was to advocate insurrection; to openly declare revolution. I am certain when the disciples asked to learn to pray that this was not what they were expecting. But the phrasing is important. Not "come and help us set up our kingdom", or "set up my kingdom" — Jesus has forgone that temptation in the desert already. It is God's initiation, design and not ours. We do not determine the principals or practices. Yet, so often, individual churches, denominations or groups of Christians design their own pseudo-kingdoms and pursue them intensely. We must relinquish control so that we are *non-authoritative* participants in His kingdom.

"Give us bread". God not only offers sustenance but abundance. He gave so that each may gather according to their need but, as these Galileans knew well, there were hungry people. Nonetheless, these men had seen a surprising and miraculous demonstration of how abundance could be found even in a desert: When Jesus fed the five thousand it surely pricked their imaginations reminding them of Israel's history. Surprise is the key piece to this. We may not have expectations of the provision. When Israel saw the bread in the desert they asked "What is it?", which became its name: Manna. Whilst we may believe that we can design and conceive of what is needed God will surprise us, intentionally. To remind us that this is about his will and ordering; must expect to be surprised and so be *non-prescriptive* in our expectations.

Waxing the Board

Israel, as a community, had failsafes written into their constitution to prevent systemic poverty and perpetual debt. These release laws should have been vital but there is little to suggest they were ever fully enacted. The word redistribution must have¹ been too much for their economists as well as ours. Nonetheless, Jesus touches upon the principles of release within this prayer. This is an important idea for servanthood: releasing debts. When we do something for another we can log it in our mind's ledger. When we feel we have received adequate recompense we may expunge the debt. But many still carry around a list of those still in their debt; those who have not yet adequately reciprocated. And that list becomes a point of bitterness in our hearts that can consume a person. We must become *non-commercial*: not offering with the expectation of repayment, not serving with a condition of remuneration. It is as counter to our intuitions as it must have been to those hearing Jesus teach this prayer.

Why would God lead us into temptation? I think our misreading and unhelpful understandings of Genesis 3 have caused the importance of this phrase to slip past us. Bearing God's name can lead us towards violence. If you do not agree then look towards history: Constantine claimed that he was to conquer in this sign, or under His name. The Inquisition was determined to establish orthodoxy in His name. The KKK have used His name to justify their terrible actions. Those believing they are doing God's will have frequently been led to acts of horrific violence and "othering". In our own era we have seen the church marginalise and exclude groups in its desire to maintain orthodoxy. This is why we must adopt a posture of being *non-evangelical*. We must not create an idol of our orthodoxy believing that it must be imposed upon all because, as this always has, it will lead us to unspeakable violence. It is easy to create a boundary around these extreme examples and say that we could never behave that way, but we have seen ugly, divisive polarisation in our churches where team A has "othered" team B, and team B has declared team A unorthodox or heretical. We can become so fixated with the idols we create that we fail to see God in the people around us.

Getting in the Water

This prayer, as well as teaching much more, chimes with our five principles of servanthood and offers a subversive and freeing way to be in the world that, in a beautiful cyclical truth, can only be maintained by prayer.

Waxing the board well is a beautiful and simple analogy for prayer. Prayer is simple, repetitive, meditative, and reflective. When waxing the board you are doing something very simple, you repeat motions again and again which stills the mind and allows reflection to occur.

However, both can be rushed. There are times when we neglect what we know to be beneficial and necessary choosing instead to rush it in the car park before jumping in. In surfing and in ministry this often results in falling on your face. I remember one of my early hurried attempts at waxing the board I neglected to do the rails of the board (the edges) meaning each time I attempted to hold them whilst getting to my feet my hands slipped and I fell on my face. The frustration of missing almost every wave because I had neglected 2 inches of board was unbearable.

This is not to say that if you pray everything will go smoothly. That is an odd sort of prosperity gospel that is unhelpful and dangerous. There are times when I have put a lot of time into preparations and prayer and still nothing has worked. Instead, prayer enables the connection, control, and poise. Just like the layer of the wax stopping to board being slippery, prayer keeps us grounded and centred. It won't change the ocean and it won't change the waves; but it will help in how we may respond to them.

In this way it is *non-authoritative*. Prayer is yielding and admitting that we are not in control. We cannot command what is going to happen. Even with all our experience and expertise we must simply be prepared; grounded and humble.

Practice centring prayer.

Find your Spot

Every surfer has their favourite break; the place where waves are often the right size, breaking the right way. Beaches can be full of difficulties and dangers. We will talk about rip tides and currents later, but for now we'll think about rocks and obstacles. Surfing in shallow waters is pretty risky. There is a good chance you will catch the board on something, or, when you wipe out you'll almost definitely collide with something.

Luke 6: 46–49

Two Builders

> [46] Why do you keep on saying that I am your Lord, when you refuse to do what I say? [47] Anyone who comes and listens to me and obeys me [48] is like someone who dug down deep and built a house on solid rock. When the flood came and the river rushed against the house, it was built so well that it didn't even shake. [49] But anyone who hears what I say and doesn't obey me is like someone whose house wasn't built on solid rock. As soon as the river rushed against that house, it was smashed to pieces!

Aside from it being very annoying, the children's song that springs into most of our minds when we read this passage (if it didn't then be thankful and do yourself a favour by not finding it to listen to) does not serve the point Jesus is trying to make overly well. Firstly we must note who Jesus is addressing: those that call him Lord. Often this parable is used to reinforce smugness about being in the in-crowd, those that have built on the rock of being on Jesus side. But it is to those that he is speaking, and quite abruptly at that: "You call me Lord and yet ignore what I am saying". He entreats us to dig down deep to find that which is worth constructing our lives upon. For many of us this will mean a difficult process of hauling heavy, well-established, undisturbed wet sand from deep within our imaginations.

The number will vary from person to person but a large percentage of the decisions and determinations we make in our day-to-day life will be based on things we have inherited from places other than Jesus' teaching: Our cultural setting will perhaps have constructed our identity around issues of class, ethnicity — perhaps most strongly the tribe of Church we come from. Our political lives will have been profoundly shaped by Western democracy to the point where many believe there is no viable alternative to this model. Our economic lives will have been strongly influenced by the consumer-capitalism that is maintained around us. Our social lives will form our opinions and viewpoints as we create for ourselves echo-chambers of friends and groups who share our thinking. And our spiritual lives will be a tangled mess of inherited "isms" particular to ourselves and a few others within our tribe. All of this is the wet sand which must be dug out. Little of it makes for good building material. If we do not undertake this difficult digging then we had better be ready to live in the shed because when crisis comes it may be the only place left: a diminished, small, damp reality cluttered with discarded ephemera. Or we can do the difficult work and build a house that is light, open, and beautiful where we can welcome others and be in His presence.

Surfing in shallow spots is often a temptation, particularly if the swell is big and there is a long paddle out. It can seem easier just to catch the already broken waves amongst the surf in the shallows; to go for easy wins. We will come back to some of this later, but for now it is about picking a spot. Or, rather, being led to a spot. Looking beyond the immediate and what seems so readily available to where we are really called to be — out in the deeper water where the waves are clear and clean rather than broken and finished. By the time waves reach the shallow water their energy is spent and their structure is gone — there really is not anything left to surf. And the danger is that if-and-when you come off the board you will hit the deck pretty easily.

Those who are looking for a place to minister or serve must be attentive to the depth. You are often in shallow water where a culture or orthodoxy has been so engrained and enforced that it creates tribalism. These can feel like really welcoming and friendly places; a strong institution or community that cares for one another and shares life together. But probe a little deeper and you may find that this friendliness is based on being part of the tribe and adopting the culture or orthodoxy. I inherited a youth congregation before going into full-time ministry where the tribalism was pretty strong. One of the first things I started was a Saturday kick about with the young people living around the church building. Out of curiosity I think, some of these guys came along one Sunday evening to our service. I expected them to be welcomed but a small number of long-term members of the congregation were quite hostile. They understood that we were a church who cared about our community but limited that to those who had the t-shirts and had been there for a while. Their understanding of church was just too shallow.

Similarly, but almost at the other end, some of the longer-established members who were maturing in faith started visiting other churches and connecting with other Christian groups. Sadly, as they did some less mature members became hostile towards them, accusing them of leaving, or being traitors. I had been encouraging the progression as you cannot really be part of a youth congregation when you are no longer a youth, but I had not anticipated the pain and challenge it would present those journeying beyond the boundaries of the tribe. Once again, the shallow waters presented some unanticipated but obvious problems. We needed to get out to deeper waters to really connect with what God was up to rather than remaining in the shallows of our tribe.

Getting in the Water

To say that we need to pick our spot is unhelpful which I why this section is entitled Finding your Spot. Perhaps it should read Being led to your spot. Servanthood is *non-prescriptive*: we can rarely just glance at the ocean and pick the bit we like. We need to be aware of the depth, the potential obstacles, where and how the waves break on this particular beach. It takes time to discern, guidance from those who have surfed there before and the intuitions we are cultivating. In the same way must be attentive to where we are ministering, growing in our awareness and being open to advice. Rather than picking our spot we must, ultimately, be led to where to serve. We must become an obedient servant.

Practice Discernment.

Paddling Out

Paddle Through

Paddling out is a difficult bit of surfing. Surfing happens on the waves right at the back before they are broken and the energy and structure is gone. Polynesians, who were the first to surf, called it "sliding on waves" because the intention is that you slide down the front of the wave — this is pretty impossible once a wave has broken because that front surface is gone. So, paddling through the broken waves, the surf, the white churning waters and then through the point where they are actually breaking is what is needed. There are sometimes clever ways to avoid these — although we will talk about these later. It can be a terrifying paddle. Mistime your paddling and you find yourself watching as a wave at full height and power crashes onto you. But something really important is happening on the paddle out. You are learning the nature of the waves: Their size, frequency, where they are breaking, how often the sets (waves come in sets) are coming, if there are any winds around. All this information is going to be important when you start catching these waves.

Luke 1: 26–38 and 46–55

An angel tells about the birth of Jesus and Mary's song of praise

²⁶ One month later God sent the angel Gabriel to the town of Nazareth in Galilee ²⁷ with a message for a virgin

named Mary. She was engaged to Joseph from the family of King David. [28] The angel greeted Mary and said, "You are truly blessed! The Lord is with you."

[29] Mary was confused by the angel's words and wondered what they meant. [30] Then the angel told Mary, "Don't be afraid! God is pleased with you, [31] and you will have a son. His name will be Jesus. [32] He will be great and will be called the Son of God Most High. The Lord God will make him king, as his ancestor David was. [33] He will rule the people of Israel forever, and his kingdom will never end."

[34] Mary asked the angel, "How can this happen? I am not married!"

[35] The angel answered, "The Holy Spirit will come down to you, and God's power will come over you. So your child will be called the holy Son of God. [36] Your relative Elizabeth is also going to have a son, even though she is old. No one thought she could ever have a baby, but in three months she will have a son. [37] Nothing is impossible for God!"

[38] Mary said, "I am the Lord's servant! Let it happen as you have said." And the angel left her.

[46] Mary said:
With all my heart I praise the Lord,
[47] and I am glad because of God my Saviour.
[48] He cares for me, his humble servant.
From now on, all people will say God has blessed me.
[49] God All-Powerful has done great things for me, and his
    name is holy.
[50] He always shows mercy to everyone who worships him.
[51] The Lord has used his powerful arm to scatter those who
    are proud.
[52] He drags strong rulers from their thrones
and puts humble people in places of power.
[53] God gives the hungry good things to eat,
and sends the rich away with nothing.
[54] He helps his servant Israel and is always merciful to his
    people.
[55] The Lord made this promise to our ancestors,

to Abraham and his family forever!"

The particulars of Jesus birth are well-travelled roads that we probably do not need to journey down here. The points we could draw about Mary's commitment to becoming socially excluded, about her age & marital status etc will be drawn from other passages. Instead, from these two excerpts of Luke's birth narrative we see a parallel with paddling out. As she goes, Mary demonstrates an increasing awareness of God's activity.

Understandably, at first Mary is overwhelmed and dismayed: I am not sure the angel's first announcement really helps as it is, to say the least, obtuse. "You are blessed, the Lord is with you" ... OK, great. Thanks... anything else? Luke places the announcement in the mouth of the angel Gabriel, symbolising to Luke's audience that despite all that has befallen them as followers of the Way, God remains with them as a presence to strengthen them. Gabriel means "God is my strength" and would have been well-recognised as a representative of God's protection for them personally. Paddling out takes strength — you are moving the board through the water for quite a distance. Similarly, to reach the place you are to serve can also take some time, strength, and resilience. I can think of several friends and co-conspirators who have had very specific callings to places and ministries but the journey there has been fraught with difficulties: from practical issues of housing and relocations to difficulties with health to challenges with institutions and permissions. Along the way all have needed, and thankfully found, God's generosity and sustenance. Luke names Gabriel within the narrative as a reminder to those commencing their journeys that, like Mary, in being willing to serve they can expect to be strengthened for it.

And, in a very real but different way, we are all called to be Mary: Mary, through her service, brought a tangible, knowable God into the world.

Mary's first understanding of God's activity is that it is something that is going to affect her personally. Notice, in the little she says to Gabriel, her language indicates she is considering the impact of God's activity on her. "How can this happen? *I* am not married?" and "*I* am the Lord's servant".

At the start of the paddle we are intensely aware that it is something we are undertaking. *We* are commencing *our* session. But very quickly, as we get further out, we become aware that God is doing quite a lot already. We are surrounded by waves; we watch their beauty and power. We, perhaps, see others already out on them. Slowly our minds shift to realise that we are joining in with something greater than ourselves.

In Mary's hymn of praise that realisation is made clear. Her language shifts from being focussed on what she will experience and do, to the bigger story of what God is doing. It is littered with His name; He, Lord, God. As she has got further into the depths of what is happening, of what God is doing, she has become aware of a much more exciting reality. This is not just about the son she will have but about the redemption and recreation of the world. Luke intentionally composes her hymn with notes from Hannah's song [1 Samuel 2] and chords from Psalm 113, which is traditionally sung during Passover to knit together that Mary has become aware that through her offspring liberation will come. In her hymn she describes the three primal tasks of the Lord; to embody justice, mercy, and faithfulness. The hymn is written in the present and past tense; which seems odd for a woman anticipating the birth of her child and looking forward to what God will do through him. It is easy not to notice this, but it communicates something quite profound: Mary's confidence in God's activity. She has begun her important journey certain of what will come to pass as a result. This confidence, I believe, comes from knowing the fidelity of God's activity well.

As we journey out, through the waves, we learn the rhythm, cadences, amplitude of God's activity as we paddle through it. This is essential learning. Feeling a wave is it passes beneath you will help you pin-point where and how to drop in (catch it). As we approach any ministry or service we do well to pay attention to what is already happening. We cannot remain in that phase of it being about *us* and *our* activity but must shift to seeing the bigger picture of what God is up to. There are some simple and practical ways to do this. We must pray, discern, and seek the Spirit through contemplation, meditation, and dwelling in Scripture. These will undoubtedly put us in touch with the rhythm and cadence of what God is doing. But we can also take a very practical leaf from Mary's book: go and speak to someone with a similar calling who is perhaps a bit further along.

On-the-whole I have been blessed with good colleagues in the towns in which I have ministered. One of the first things I do when I arrive is try to arrange to have coffee with as many of them as possible to hear about the town and what is already happening. In a very practical way this stops my ego in its tracks — before I have time to think *I* am going to do this-and-that I hear that God is already doing this-and-that. Or that this-and-that has been done for several years already. Or, excitingly, that they have sensed a need for this-and-that but have not yet found a co-conspirator. What is saddening is when these conversations become about establishing boundaries: *We* already do that, *I have* got a great programme for that in place [we will return to this towards the end when we talk about others in the water]. The emphasis is generally on *we* or *I* when this happens, indicating to me a church or leader who is still in the immaturity of the first few moments of their paddle out.

Servanthood is about de-centralising the *I* or *we*, removing the ego from what we are doing. In this way it is *non-authoritative*: We are not making the decisions about what should be done and by who; we are not the instigators or initiators of activity; instead we are participating, submitting, yielding to what God is already doing — and probably has been doing for some time. And we may be in the lovely position to be able to lend something fresh or support some tired hands within it.

Practice Unity.

Paddle Beyond

THERE IS A POINT, PARTICULARLY when surfing larger swells, or when waves are in close sets, that during the paddle out you feel as though you have hit a boundary. There is a wall of water before you, looming above you. There are two techniques to get past this; duck dive — essentially forcing the board downwards underneath the water to punch through the other side. This is only really possible with short boards as long boards have too greater volume to be forced under the surface like this. The other option is hoping you can time it correcting and paddling over the top. Neither is easy. This threshold can be difficult to pass. But to truly surf it is essential. There are those who have done everything right, but because they cannot get beyond this boundary they never catch the rides that are calling them.

Luke 8: 26-33

Jesus heals a demon-possessed man

[26] They sailed to the region of the Gerasenes, which is across the lake from Galilee. [27] When Jesus stepped ashore, he was met by a demon-possessed man from the town. For a long time this man had not worn clothes or lived in a house, but had lived in the tombs. [28] When he saw Jesus, he cried out and fell at his feet, shouting at the top of his voice, "What do you want with me, Jesus, Son of the Most High God? I beg you, don't torture

me!" ²⁹ For Jesus had commanded the impure spirit to come out of the man. Many times it had seized him, and though he was chained hand and foot and kept under guard, he had broken his chains and had been driven by the demon into solitary places.

³⁰ Jesus asked him, "What is your name?"

"Legion," he replied, because many demons had gone into him. ³¹ And they begged Jesus repeatedly not to order them to go into the Abyss.

³² A large herd of pigs was feeding there on the hillside. The demons begged Jesus to let them go into the pigs, and he gave them permission. ³³ When the demons came out of the man, they went into the pigs, and the herd rushed down the steep bank into the lake and was drowned.

First we will need a bit of geography, then a bit of history and then we may be able to gain some of the rich teaching contained in this entirely bizarre episode of Luke's gospel.

The region of the Garasenes was on the east side of Lake Galilee in an area known as the Decapolis: this was an area containing ten (deca) cities (polis) that was an autonomous region within the Roman Empire. Surrounded by Semitic peoples the Decapolis, as indicated by its name, was the centre for Greek and Roman culture within this area of intersection of modern-day Israel, Jordan, Syria, and Lebanon. They spoke a different language, worshipped different gods and their communities and society was structured and operated in an entirely different way to that of their close neighbours in the Galilee where Jesus and the disciples had set out from. This is not to say there were not Jewish inhabitants, as there were in most populated areas in the ancient near east, but it was a starkly different culture.

For the disciples, mostly young men who have grown up in the small, thoroughly Jewish, fishing and farming communities of the Galilee crossing to the other side of the Lake was leaving the known world. An imprecise, but perhaps helpful, analogy would be the well-travelled trope of rural kid visiting the big city. However, this has its limitations; there are many other boundaries being traversed by Jesus and his students. Foremost, that they are heading to a predominantly Gentile population. What could they possibly be doing there? Jesus is drawing his disciple out of their security, familiarity, assumptions; out of their primitive theological frameworks, their conceptions of God, their understandings of Scripture — in every way he is taking them beyond well-established boundaries. I am certain that as they travelled over the lake there was a good amount of fear and anxiety accompanying the curiosity and excitements and adrenaline.

When I began as a Youth Pastor at the youth congregation I was pretty much welcomed as you would expect: Some hostility from those who were deeply committed to the previous leader [It was an awkward transition because he had been a full-time, fully trained youth worker at the church and I was a nobody with little experience who was going to do it part-time], but generally I was met with curiosity and a measure of respect. However, part of the role was to run a late-night youth drop in on a Friday night. The church was situated amongst parts of London well-known for gang violence and the drop in intended to provide a safe place for guys who may be involved. This was my analogous experience. Expecting to be welcomed in a similar way to how the congregation had met me; part hostility, part curiosity, part tokenistic respect I was entirely ignored. I mean literally ignored. When I spoke, the guys who had come in were completely non-responsive and just carried on their conversations and games of pool.

It is often the way that, in servanthood, we are taken out of where we were comfortable and secure and established. Servanthood is *non-authoritative*. It is difficult to be an authority where no-one knows your name, or who you are, or even the language you speak. Where, not only are you not recognised for your position, but you are not accorded the usual respect or treatment it has offered you in the past. This may benefit us in quickly stripping the ego away, but it can be a very difficult boundary to traverse: Particularly if we have been reared in an environment where position has afforded de-facto respect and admiration. Servanthood is non-prescriptive in that we must leave that which has been the norm — the accepted and the known — for something new.

Leaving our known world can be difficult and will cause some to turn back and head for shallower waters.

In 66ce, after Jesus but before Luke's gospel was composed, during the Jewish war with Rome, Lucius Annius, a Roman commander, led his troops to Geresa to slaughter the men, pillage the city and then burn the homes of those they had killed or driven off. Despite being similarly cultured to Rome we must not forget that the Decapolis was, like the Galilee, under the oppression of a highly militarised Empire. Although these events come after Jesus' life there is no way that Luke, as a skilled author, is not making a point within the narrative. When Jesus arrives on the shore he is met by a man possessed who refers to himself as Legion, a word obviously linked to the Roman military apparatus. Perhaps Luke is illustrating for us the effects that social, economic, political, physical, and spiritual oppression have on a population. I would be lying if I said I did not see parallels within the towns I work in; people who have lost hope, dignity, and their personhood as victims of a less overt but similarly dehumanising imperial oppression. Taking up servanthood is unlikely to mean settling into a life of quietness; we are drawn towards those who are under the boot of an oppressor; be it unemployment, poor housing, homelessness, domestic abuse, human trafficking, poverty, miseducation, maltreatment etc. etc. In this way, as we cross the boundary into the deep we are crossing to a place where we will confront the empire.

It is the pigs that make the story truly odd. Augustine concluded it merely demonstrated how Christians do not hold duties towards animals but I suspect, as a Roman, he may have missed the subtle point being made here. The spirits flee into the pigs which in turn flee into the water and are drowned. If we scan our knowledge of Scripture for a parallel we can recall another significant time when the military apparatus of an oppressive empire is drowned in a sea within an action of liberation: The Exodus (where we must so often go back to). Piecing this together makes more sense of this story that at first reading is so strange.

Once freed and in his right mind Legion is keen to remain with Jesus and his disciples. Yet, Jesus says no. Here, again, we see a *non-evangelical* principle at work. Jesus is not seeking to amass a crowd. Even when tempted with a foreign, diverse person who could powerfully testify to Jesus' power by showing the physical scars from which he had been saved Jesus says no. This is the counter-instinctive *non-commercialism* for many who have lived within a church growth culture where diversity and powerful testimonies of transformed lives were accrued like commodities. Yet, despite the man's begging, Jesus says no.

Instead he sends him home to share his story. Without helping him refine the story, without ensuring he makes the correct theological points, without helping him to understand all the Scriptural and Doctrinal tenets that undergird his story, without training him to deliver it in the most socially acceptable and culturally relevant way, without coaching him on converting others, without teaching him how to structure and shape his story; he is just sent. For a moment consider how the disciples may have felt about this. They are working day-in day-out to do as their Rabbi does so that they may, eventually, be commissioned into service with all the requisite skills and experience — yet Jesus just sends this man. Their must surely have been a little resentment towards him or astonishment at Jesus' behaviour. Servanthood may be *non-professional*. Those who have not been helped, taught, trained, coached, and moulded by seminaries and training courses and professional qualifications, by the pure power of their testimony and the authenticity of their transformation, are enough.

For a couple of years I was friends with a charismatic, entrepreneurial, and hospitable man who when I first met was homeless. Slowly we worked on that and eventually, together with support from other churches and agencies, he was housed. Sharing that first cup of tea in his little bedsit was a real privilege. He had always professed a faith and wanted to be baptised. This was arranged and I did some work with him before as traditionally he would give his testimony. I felt quite responsible for Steve. I had vouched for him on several occasions and taken some real risks. I had journeyed with him. And my colleagues and friends in the other churches knew this. So when he spoke in some ways they would register what he said against me. I was eager to ensure he did not say anything too unsettling. In fact, if I am really honest I wanted to use his testimony to further my own agenda about inclusion and compassion that I felt was lacking in the local church. After some time trying to shape and refine his story Steve was becoming exasperated: "Can't I just tell them what happened?" Steve's story was all he needed. And so we agreed that is what he would tell them. The only condition I made was that he try not to swear too violently ... he was unsuccessful.

This has been a longer section that usual so may help to recapture some of our key points:

Servanthood is *non-prescriptive*: Jesus and his disciples left what was known, understood and comfortable as they crossed the sea for the Decapolis.

This positioned them as *non-authoritative*: They were unknown, without authority or even respect. In fact, the only person that greeted them was the city's outcast.

Jesus responds to the man's desire to join them with 1) a *non-evangelical* principle by denying his request to accompany them and 2) a *non-commercial* principle by not capitalising on the man and his story.

Rather, Jesus commissions him as a *non-professional*: The man is just sent out without training or checking his theology is ok or that his strategy is sound. He is sent to share his story.

Practice Labyrinth Prayer.

Paddle out and Wait

When you paddle out you are travelling against the waves, through the surf until you are behind the point the waves are breaking and peeking. It can be a long paddle. It can be tiring and on some beaches can be quite a distance. Yet, the whole way you are anticipating the rides, seeing other surfers carve and dance down the line. When you finally reach the back it can be tempting to dive straight at the first wave that comes but good surfers wait. There may still be some things to learn now you are out there. You may still need to wait for the ocean to present something new to you. Your arms will need a brief rest before they can paddle to catch anything.

Luke 1: 8-20

[8] One day Zechariah's group of priests were on duty, and he was serving God as a priest. [9] According to the custom of the priests, he had been chosen to go into the Lord's temple that day and to burn incense, [10] while the people stood outside praying.

[11] All at once an angel from the Lord appeared to Zechariah at the right side of the altar. [12] Zechariah was confused and afraid when he saw the angel. [13] But the angel told him:

Don't be afraid, Zechariah! God has heard your prayers. Your wife Elizabeth will have a son, and you must name him John. [14] His birth will make you very happy, and many people will be glad. ¹⁵ Your son will be a great servant of the Lord. He must never drink wine or beer, and the power of the Holy Spirit will be with him from the time he is born.

¹⁶ John will lead many people in Israel to turn back to the Lord their God. ¹⁷ He will go ahead of the Lord with the same power and spirit that Elijah had. And because of John, parents will be more thoughtful of their children. And people who now disobey God will begin to think as they ought to. That is how John will get people ready for the Lord.

¹⁸ Zechariah said to the angel, "How will I know this is going to happen? My wife and I are both very old."

¹⁹ The angel answered, "I am Gabriel, God's servant, and I was sent to tell you this good news. ²⁰ You have not believed what I have said. So you will not be able to say a thing until all this happens. But everything will take place when it is supposed to."

It is all too easy to read Zachariah's imposed silence as a punishment for his unfaithfulness or for his doubting; but I believe this is too simplistic a reading and plays unhelpfully into the old Christian troupe of faith being in contradiction to doubt. The opposite of faith is not doubt, the opposite of faith is certainty. Instead, Zachariah's silence offers us something more important.

Luke places Zachariah and Elizabeth into his narrative as a recapitulation of another important couple in Israel's history; Abraham and Sarah. Advanced in years and without a son the resemblance is an important chime for us to indicate that the story Luke is going to tell us is about YHWH's action and intervention in the world to summon a people to an alternate life. Luke also picks up some of the playful comedy from the Genesis narrative that we so often miss in our pious, or perhaps pompous, reading of Scripture with Zachariah making gesticulations and signs to try and describe the experience he has just had.

He has been told that the Messiah is imminent; that the liberation of all peoples is about to begin and that the Kingdom of God is arriving. In a few brief moments of incredible exchange Zachariah travels the whole journey; personal calling to fatherhood, commission to nurture one who will lead the people, responsibility to cultivate hope that Kingdom is indeed close. Were Zachariah not literally dumb-struck the temptation for him to burst out of the Temple and dive straight into proclamation would have been too great to resist.

And so, his silence comes as a gift. As a means by which he can take a breath, wait, gain a deeper awareness of what is happening. Like Mary he will need to go from understanding the personal implications to comprehending the larger picture of God's activity.

After paddling out, beyond the threshold of the breaking waves, I, and many others, pause. We stop. All that effort and struggle can be seen as having a singular intention; to get surfing. But we know that we have been surfing the whole time. Surfing is not simply the act of standing on a board; it is more than that. It is everything that happens; from preparing to get into the water, through the paddle out, during the catching and riding of waves all the way out to getting back in the car. There are a variety of things happening that are all surfing.

Nonetheless, we have reached an important point within the whole. We are now there; at the waves edge, ready to turn the board and drop in to our first ride. But instead we stop. Often sitting up on the board we take a moment. For me personally this is a really important moment in every session. It is chance to appreciate the beauty of where I am and chance to deepen my awareness of what is happening around me. It is only at this point we really see who else is in the water and what they are doing. It is only at this point that you can enjoy seeing God's activity unobscured by the efforts you are making to get involved.

Often we can make our call to servanthood highly individualised and turn our paddling out journeys into melodramas centred entirely on ourselves: Our burning bush experience, our trial in the wilderness, the burning coal touched to our lips, our leaving our nets and boats to follow him. We relegate everything else we have been doing to insignificance against this new reality of ministry. It is a dangerous thing to begin our ministry in such a mindset — we

Paddle out and Wait

will quickly become the messiah we believe is needed rather than serving the one who is already at work. We will quickly become entrenched in our ego; making our plans and projects our priorities. This isn't helped by the fact that when we do arrive we are suddenly opened to a whole new language of impact measurement and story capturing and statistical collation and development tools that seek to quantify and qualify what we are doing. These are not necessarily bad in of themselves but can trip us into feeding our ego with either a false sense of accomplishment or painful insecurity. I am glad we have almost left it behind, but at least it was quicker and simpler when we could all just compare congregation size to establish how well-endowed we were as ministers.

The pause is vital. Paddle out and then wait. I suspect it is why older and wiser denominations send their newly ordained ministers on a retreat before they assume their responsibilities: So they will stop. The whole process of being publicly acknowledged, welcomed, and given a role stokes the fires of the ego like nothing else; surrounded by friends and family and imbibed with a sense of unique purpose and calling we make ourselves the solution to the deficits we will undoubtedly confront where we are being sent. Waiting will give us time to set all this aside. Silence will prevent us telling ourselves that it is true. Pausing will suffocate the flames of our ego perhaps enough so that we do not burn ourselves and those we are amongst too quickly.

In this way servanthood is *non-commercial*. The commercial imagination would want to capitalize on all that investment as quickly as possible. It would want hurried and rapid activity, instant results, immediate transformations. It can plunge the servant into frantic and fruitless activity all too soon. Zachariah is gifted time to simply rest in what has happened without describing or giving language to it — just to witness to it to himself: "I'm here, this has happened, look at the beauty of God's activity in the world". To be unhurried in what we are doing is a similar gift. To not dive in straight away is vital. Instead, sit and be still and silent. Wait.

Practice Retreat.

You in the Water

It's not about You

Surfing is unusual amongst sports in that surfers are far more willing to credit the sea; acknowledge we are participating with something bigger than ourselves. When I climb mountains or when I mountain bike trails it is entirely about what I do. Within surfing there is a culture of acknowledgment and gratitude that we are joining in with something amazing that the sea is doing.

Luke 17: 5-6

[5] The apostles said to the Lord, "Make our faith stronger!"
[6] Jesus replied:
"If you had faith no bigger than a tiny mustard seed, you could tell this mulberry tree to pull itself up, roots and all, and to plant itself in the ocean. And it would!"

There is a succinct truth and simple application of this; that it is not about you. Which is quick to hear but slow to learn. Jesus is teaching his disciples that it is not about them. The verse is often used as an encouragement or affirmation to new Christians but perhaps this slightly misconstrues it. The common interpretation is that no matter how small your faith you can do amazing things. It is tantamount to the teaching that is so often erroneously drawn out from David and Goliath — a small thing can conquer a big thing. It is not that this is untrue. But with both passages the interpretation is centred on you, and it's not about you. The story of David is not about you; it is a story about how one from the line of

David will stand against a giant military oppressor and be victorious in an unexpected way; standing as one on behalf of others and in complete vulnerability. David and Goliath prefigure the Easter story and yet we make it about our problems at work, or our financial situations or any other relatively trivial personal concerns. We can do this because we make it about us.

Similarly, Jesus is not teaching the disciples that if they just try really hard they will surely succeed against the odds. He is teaching that it is not about how powerful our faith in God is or is not, but about how powerful the God we have faith in is. Jesus is trying to decentralise us from the story; trying to remove the ego.

In our tendency towards *professionalism* we want to be seen to be competent or powerful but it is not about us. We may only surf because the wave generously allows us to. It is the wave's strength, speed and structure that enables anything at all to happen. If you don't believe me, try standing on a surfboard on a flat sea. This moves counter to the objectives, strategies and effectiveness that are tenets of *professionalism*. Similarly it contradicts the notions of control, power, and self-initiation of *authority*. Servanthood readily acknowledges that we act on behalf of another; that it is something else that is at work. The church, like surfing, must cultivate a culture of acknowledgment and gratitude that we are joining in with something amazing that God is doing.

Practice Gratitude.

It's not about Standing up

For those who are not surfers this will make little sense. Most reduce surfing to getting stood up on the board as you ride a wave. After all, that is what you see in the photos, videos, adverts, posters etc. That is what you may have observed when you have glanced at surfers from the beach. But it is not about standing up. It is not even that the standing up is the culmination of a process or the end goal. Standing up is just one part of the whole thing. The paddle out, the waiting, the positioning, all that went on before you got in the water; it is not all in service of the point you drop in and get stood up. They are all just parts of a whole experience. Admittedly riding the wave may be the most thrilling and exciting; but riding a wave and standing up are not the same thing. New surfers, if they can decentralise standing up and work on all the other bits as well, will find their enjoyment of surfing, and ability, will improve rapidly. But for those who just want to get stood up, they may find their experiences limiting and frustrating.

Luke 9: 51-56

A Samaritan Village Refuses to Receive Jesus

⁵¹ Not long before it was time for Jesus to be taken up to heaven, he made up his mind to go to Jerusalem. ⁵² He sent some messengers on ahead to a Samaritan village to get things ready for him. ⁵³ But he was on his way

to Jerusalem, so the people there refused to welcome him. ⁵⁴ When the disciples James and John saw what was happening, they asked, "Lord, do you want us to call down fire from heaven to destroy these people?"

⁵⁵ But Jesus turned and corrected them for what they had said, ⁵⁶ Then they all went on to another village.

This episode is part of a passage in Luke that occurs along the last leg of Jesus' journey towards Jerusalem. We will look at the other episodes in time; with squabbles amongst disciples about who is the greatest and others asking to follow Jesus and being disappointed. However, none of the other passages are quite as odd as this. "Do you want us to call down fire?" By this point James and John have been on the road with Jesus for some time. We can be forgiven for wondering how on earth they would ask such a question; how could they ask if Jesus wanted something so out-of-character, something so violent? But our incredulity towards the two may be slightly unwarranted if we fail to piece together the whole puzzle.

If we track back just a short way within the chapter of Luke's gospel [v18–21] we have the exchange where Jesus asks, "who do you say I am?" The disciples' response is telling. We almost always focus on Peter's insight that Jesus is the Messiah but the other responses are important and interesting — in particular the thought that he might be Elijah, who many believed would return and prepare the way for the Messiah. James and John, who are named as Sons of Thunder in Mark's gospel, are fishermen from the Galilee. They are rough, strong and have grown up under crushing oppression from the Roman Empire and cruel contempt from Israel's elites. They interpret Jesus' activity through a lens of violent, yet righteous, retribution and so naturally understand him as a recapitulation, if not return, of Elijah.

Luke is sensitive to their understanding and perhaps some similarity in outlook between James and John and his own audience who were facing persecution from within and without. So, Luke carefully demonstrates Jesus' distinction from Elijah for the reader, using parallelism to highlight the dissimilarities. Both will

It's not about Standing up

be "taken up" [Luke 9:51 and 2 Kings 2:9-12], but whereas Elijah calls down fire [2 Kings 1], Jesus fiercely rejects this. And whereas Elijah allows Elisha to return to his family before following [1 Kings 19:19-21] Jesus warns followers not to look back from their ploughshare and rejects those with business at home to attend to first [Luke 9: 57-62].

Nonetheless, James and John see what their lens allows them and remain fixed in their hope that Jesus will, like Elijah, lead them to violent confrontation with those do not regard this man of God in the proper fashion; be it this Samaritan village or the Roman Empire. They refer to the incident in 2 Kings 1 where King Ahaziah, having fallen out of his window, turns to a god other than YHWH for healing. Elijah condemns him, yet it is not this that ignites Elijah's flaming retribution; it is when Ahaziah dispatches officers to order him down from the mountain his is sitting on. It seems that when they fail to accord him the proper respect of a prophet that his pyromania is provoked.

James and John are not just out for a mindless brawl, but seeking the position, prestige and progeny that would come from victory. In this episode their retribution is fuelled by their desire for Jesus, and by association themselves, to be accorded the proper position and respect deserving of men of God. They want to be noticed and recognised as being that which they aspire to. Jesus rejects this. I suspect not just for its violence; after all, he is willing to concede that it will be Capernaum will have a worse fate than Tyre or Sidon. Instead, I think James and John's question is met with rebuke because their anger towards the Samaritan town comes from their ego being affronted. Their motivation was that they were not recognised, welcomed, and treated as men of power and Jesus is working incredible hard to instil humility, non-violence, and submission in his disciples.

I was going to say that I am sure not many in ministry have desired to call down fire on a group of people, but I am not sure I believe that. Nonetheless, we may have all shared James and John's frustrations with not being recognised, of not being accepted and treated in a particular manner. Our ego can motivate a great desire to be noticed. We desire acknowledgment of our competency, of our activity being noticed, valued, and accredited to us. At the least we desire treatment appropriate to our position.

Problematically our structures and cultures often do not ease the relegation of our desire to be noticed and accredited and accorded the proper respect. As the *professionals* within our Christian communities we are sometimes accredited with so much power and authority it unsettles us. We are frequently placed for everyone to notice. Our activity is often drawn attention to. Even physically we cannot help but be positioned above or in front of groups of people. All of which compounds the way in which we are regarded and related to.

I remember the first time I saw someone die within my ministry. I was hurriedly invited to a house as a man was in the very final stages of cancer. The family were anxious for my arrival with the door to the house already open. The pleasantries on my arrival extraordinarily succinct as they whisked me through into the living room where a hospital bed had been placed and their very elderly father lay. With great expectancy in their eyes they led me to him to do something. I come from a tradition without a specific rite or ritual for such an occasion, which I am almost certain the family did not realise, and so I felt uniquely ill-equipped for what was expected. I had not had the opportunity to ask the family what they were expecting of me and now did not seem the most appropriate time to ask "So, what would you like me to do?" So I took the man's hand, and quietly prayed that he would know peace. Instantly the family seemed relieved as though I had uttered some incantation to make their father's death ok. The palpable tension immediately dissipated as the family relaxed in the belief I had solved the crisis. The man died almost instantly; an event that was met with a cool and collected response of putting the kettle on for a tea.

I have often reflected on this event. The power that this afforded me; the immediate respect they had for me and position they held me in by virtue of my "job": a *professional* man of God. In my reflections I have had to express my gratitude for being so perplexed and unsettled and unprepared throughout the whole episode [I had been unblocking a toilet in the church building after our parent and toddler group had blocked it when the phone had gone so was not remotely in the desirable frame of mind for such an event] that I failed to register the family's reverence for me. Should I have been more prepared, more alert, and sensitive to their reaction to me it would have undoubtedly fuelled my ego with the potent cocktail of power and position.

Service is not about being the centre of attention, being noticed or being professional: it is not about standing up. In fact, most surfing happens without anyone seeing; they are the other side of the wave, or further down the line on the wave, or concentrating on paddling out. You can watch new surfers search and search for recognition as they get stood up — eyes darting around for who has noticed them finally upright. But, rather than seeking acknowledgment we must simply enjoy what we are doing; see the beauty in it and look to do it as well as we can, not so others can appreciate or competency, but so that we can appreciate and enjoy serving well.

There is a temptation in surfing become so fixated on getting stood up that it is attempted no matter what the wave, no matter where in the water. This can lead to disasters, which we will talk about later, or lead to reduce surfing to something shallow and mundane, which we will talk about next. Getting stood up can become an indication of competency; of being a good professional. Servanthood requires that we relinquish this ego-fuelled desire. We long to show that we can do that which we have admired in others. But often it is too soon, key skills and disciplines remain untouched and unlearned. Despite not feeding my ego, the event with the dying man does demonstrate the activity of my ego. I have never admitted to that family that I had no rite or ritual to hand. I certainly did not tell them it was the first time I had been called to such an event. I wanted to appear professional, competent. I wanted to be seen to be standing up. And in doing so I compounded a belief in that family that what is needed is a quick prayer from a *professional* and peace will be secured. What would have been better would have been to enter into the grief and anxiety; walk with them through it and understand it. Instead of reducing prayer to a transaction or bargaining plea we could have explored it as a means to give language to and explore grief. Perhaps that is unrealistic for such a short event, but it demonstrates the possibilities of servanthood in contrast to the *prescriptions* of *professionalism*.

For those who are new and uncertain in ministry the pressure to look *professional* can be great and damaging. The expectation, often from ourselves, is that we should just be able to just manage; we should instinctively know what to do. In turn it creates a great anxiety for new Christians; if I cannot just do this stuff then I must not be a very good Christian. And if advice is sought it is so often unhelpful — just read your Bible, pray about it. Just let the Spirit use you. The advice is doled out as though those three things themselves were not fraught with complexity and challenge on their own.

Servanthood is about relinquishing the desire for power and position; even if it is given to us by virtue of others' assumptions about our roles. It is not about getting noticed; having competency acknowledged or power recognised. Instead it is about dwelling in the opportunities of sharing a situation with another rather than prescribing the action; about learning new truths from each event rather than recycling old reactions. It is about heeding the call to radical humility rather than calling down fire on those that do not properly regard us.

Practice Secrecy.

Knee Deep in the Surf

In the previous section I mentioned how the fixation on getting stood up can lead to reducing surfing to something shallow and mundane. If a surfer is reluctant to paddle out fully; perhaps the surf seems too messy or the swell too high. If the point is to get stood up then this can be achieved on the more manageable remains of the waves as they come into the shallows. Add to this that the surfer can stand in the water next to the board and just dive onto it when the wave arrives rather than having to paddle into it and drop in. It is how most of us begin. With a large foam board we stand knee deep in the surf dive at broken waves to stand up for a few seconds until the momentum is completely gone. It is fun, for about thirty minutes. But then it begins to feel repetitive, even monotonous. And we become increasingly aware it is not why we came. It is not really surfing.

Luke 9: 57–62

Three People Who Wanted to Be Followers

⁵⁷ Along the way someone said to Jesus, "I'll go anywhere with you!"
⁵⁸ Jesus said, "Foxes have dens, and birds have nests, but the Son of Man doesn't have a place to call his own."
⁵⁹ Jesus told someone else to come with him. But the man said, "Lord, let me wait until I bury my father."[a]

You in the Water

⁶⁰ Jesus answered, "Let the dead take care of the dead, while you go and tell about God's kingdom."
⁶¹ Then someone said to Jesus, "I want to go with you, Lord, but first let me go back and take care of things at home."
⁶² Jesus answered, "Anyone who starts ploughing and keeps looking back isn't worth a thing to God's kingdom!"

I wonder how many sermons have been preached on this passage in comparison to those preached on the calling of the first disciples. Those early stories of leaving nets and following provide many encouraging notes for those exploring their own calling; their perceived shortcomings surrounding age, schooling, background, and general refinement are all overlooked; they are compelled by a vision of Jesus; they are allowed to see themselves as becoming part of a rising movement, perhaps even prominent within it. I have spoken with Christian leaders a decade or so older than me who were told they were part of a generation that was going to "sweep this nation with the Gospel". Most look back at this thought with some humour having found fulfilling and meaningful service. Sadly though, there are some who are genuinely hurt and despondent realising that what they had imagined at the time is now unlikely to come to pass. They had been sure, perhaps like the fishermen, of how *authoritative* they would be, how *professional* they would appear and how *prescribed* their ministry would be.

This passage feels like a stark contrast to what we turn the calling narratives of the fishermen into. Yet, it is important to read and understand. And if we are going to talk to those exploring their calling it would probably help to include these verses whenever we include those other romanticised calling passages. Jesus demands a high level of commitment. The kingdom must be the paramount concern for those who follow him.

Jesus first comment, about foxes and birds is an unsettling one. Often we understand it as Jesus describing his state of homelessness. This is not an unhelpful thing for us to remember; his solidarity with, and preference for, the poor is well commented upon and important. Similarly the ensuing dependence for Jesus upon other's hospitality is worth holding in our minds. But I think there is the possibility of a more subversive political statement that Luke is drawing out. Later in Luke's Gospel Jesus refers to Herod as a fox — which must come from somewhere; perhaps it was a common nickname for Herod amongst those unimpressed by his complicity with Rome and cunning manipulation of the situation for his own gain. Rome, the heavy military presence, frequently used an eagle as a symbol: Topping standards and appearing on shields. Perhaps Jesus is drawing a contrast to clarify the kind of kingdom he is establishing. Herod has his palaces of power; Rome has its citadels and fortresses but the Son of Man is not here for that sort of power; he has no place to lay his head. Most simply, Jesus may be making those asking to follow him aware that they can expect no *place* as a result.

Next we have the comment about burying a father. It can read like an incredibly harsh denial of a son's right to be present at his father's funeral. I think it is probably worth saying I do not believe the father had just died. I once pictured this scene; a grief-stricken son stood before a funeral procession pleading with Jesus to allow him just to conclude the service and then he will be along to follow. Jesus stark remarks make little congruence with his character within this reading. When Jesus is amongst grief he tends to enter into it, sharing and demonstrating compassion. Instead this may be a comment about obligations or securities.

It was a son's duty to bury his father. Many Jews considered it as one of the most important holy obligations a son must fulfil. It would seem perfectly reasonable for someone wishing to follow Jesus to expect to fulfil this duty first. However, there is another dimension to this. It may have been that this potential follower was keen to ensure he had some security in place before following Jesus. It could be that he was asking to be allowed to continue to work the family business; ensure its profitability and when the time came, inherit the estate and business. This would give him some security; certify that he would have a place to return to if he became tired or unfulfilled by following Jesus.

You in the Water

Jesus' stern response to his request opens our eyes to what Jesus believes is of paramount importance: The Kingdom comes before any religious rite or sacred obligation or communal tradition — even that which is believed to be holy or important. Similarly Jesus is not interested in ensuring security. His wording makes clear that those working for economic security are labouring amongst the dead and that he, by contrast, is calling people to truly live.

The final exchange in this short episode seems to re-state this point but with a slightly different emphasis. It is not so much about economic security but about moving forward within a story. Those looking backwards and being concerned with what has been will fail to move in the direction they are summoned. I am not convinced that this is about locking the doors, closing the windows, and feeding the cat before going out for a trip. It is about attending to the past at the expense of the future.

These three comments make clear that following Jesus is a commitment to leave the shallows and head for the depths. The shallow waters offer security, ease, and comfort: They offer quick enjoyment as standing up is readily accessible and easily achieved. But the shallows are not where Jesus calls his followers to serve.

Looking with our lens of servanthood there are some important implications to note within these passages. The shallows offer a place where we can stand with ease; a place where we can look competent and *authoritative*. Like Herod's den or Rome's nest it is a place where we may feel empowered and secure; there is no threat from the broken waves. It is not that they are bad waves, it is just that they are spent. There is a new wave further back that is where the energy and excitement is truly to be found; where the surfing is meant to happen. Nonetheless it is easy to adopt this secure environment as our *place*. Be it established congregations, long-standing programs, or projects there is safety from these known, predictable waves; they are not bad, but fairly soon they can feel repetitive and even frustrating. And, to increase the frustration, the shallows are often very crowded waters with many other pseudo-surfers trying to catch the same broken waves.

However, leaving them is not an easy task. For ourselves, we are leaving a place in which we knew how to function. Push the board and hop on and before you know it you are standing: Great for the ego; poor for learning to surf. We can choose the right songs, include the right humorous illustrations, pick the right equipment to buy or resources to use and we will be appreciated by those in our congregations, youth clubs or small groups. But fairly quickly we will wonder if there is something deeper we are called to and these quick tricks and easy wins will become dissatisfying.

Unless you are an egomaniac. Which is a possibility, but one I doubt as you have picked up a book about being a servant which would be unusual for an egomaniac. Nonetheless it is worth a warning about. There are those who will seem to thrive on standing in the shallows, catching every wave they go for and getting stood up with ease. Those who will seem to thrive on being loved by their congregation, appreciated by their community, and admired by those they work amongst for providing the same things that have always been provided; for continuing the same repetitive motions. In a self-perpetuating cycle the more we provide what is desired, the more we will be appreciated; the more we are appreciated, the more we will provide what has earned us that appreciation. The more we hone this skill, the more we appear as an *authority* to those around us. It is a cycle we may all easily find ourselves trapped within. It is the place of security, the nest of the bird. Or, perhaps more appropriately, the fox's hole we can find ourselves eventually trapped inside.

Within my first full-time post I inherited a very small, elderly congregation that I instinctively knew was finished. Shortly after I arrived several of them died, a few moved into residential care or to be with family and some were no longer able to get to Sunday services. Before too long I had to do what I knew from the start was needed but had been reluctant to actually implement; Sunday services stopped.

I was met with a barrage of complaints from various and unexpected places. Former members, who had left before I arrived, sent emails. Members of other churches called to tell me of their disgust. I was named as a disgrace by one man in one of several letters he sent to my superiors. Many of these quoted the predictable passages of not ceasing to meet together[1] and that even where two or three are gathered[2] but the remaining congregation were at peace. They too had known it was time. We had to leave that which was an obligation, forego that which was holy and important to pursue the Kingdom: A kingdom that did not *prescribe* the traditions and duties so readily assumed as non-negotiable but instead led outwards towards the depths. I wish I had been equipped with this understanding of this passage at the time. Sadly, instead I busied myself in seeking to look so competent in other areas I could justify closing a Sunday gathering and found myself, for a time, knee deep in the shallows.

There is much talk amongst ministers of ensuring sustainability, which is probably a good idea. However, I sometimes see a contradiction between what is spoken of and Jesus' life and teaching. He rejects the would-be-follower who seeks security, or sustainability, in their own life. Jesus does not want them to secure their independence or fall-back plan. This is counter to our *commercial* imaginations. We want to have something grounded and tangible that we can return to if it gets too much. I am not talking about some off-shore account you may have, or a holiday cottage you still keep — although if you feel particularly convicted it may be worth exploring why. I mean in ministry. We keep something sustained that gives us security. When I closed the Sunday gathering I protected myself with the security of the success of our youth project. This was my bargaining chip, my bit in the bank that gave us value. I could not shoulder the thought of a value-less church. And yet, the Son of Man has no place; And yet he warns the would-be-follower that the dead are labouring amongst the dead. He is fiercely challenging our *commercialism* as he calls us out the shallows of security and sustainability.

Finally we consider Jesus' insistence that attention is focussed on what is coming and not what is past. I have never ploughed a

1. Hebrews 10:25
2. Matthew 18:20

field but my brother-in-law has been for years and is pretty good at it. He tells me that the simple truth is that as soon as you turn your head you are not looking at where you are going. I probably could have worked that out. Yet how often we devote energy and time to looking backwards for the sake of *professionalism*. We like to ensure we have a list of what we have achieved to hand; things we can point to and say "I did that". This finds its surfing parallel quite easily. We can never show anyone the wave we have surfed or the ride we had on it. You can point to a mountain and say "I climbed that". You can walk down a trail and say "I've mountain biked here". But you can never recreate a wave or adequately describe a ride; they are too fraught with nuance and subtlety about how you reacted, sensed, intuited, knew, shifted, carved. It is something that is naturally *non-professional*: It cannot be evidenced or proven; it is not measurable or even knowable. It was just something that happened that cannot be revisited.

This is not to say we should not reflect. This book is shot through with my own reflections and is hopefully eliciting some of your own. But to try and revisit, to repeat, to relive those memories is to denigrate the future that is being offered. Longing for something past is to devalue to possible future. Our desire to look back and see how we have done; be it to relive our success or fixate on our failures comes from the assumptions of *professionalism* that we are so imbibed with and yet must resist.

Servanthood entails obedience to the master, and Jesus seems to be instructing us to leave the shallows; of our places of security, of our desires for sustainability, of our memories of success and follow him to the deeper waters where we can know him more fully.

Practice the Presence.

In Too Deep

I AM A SELF-TAUGHT SURFER, which means I am full of bad habits and poor techniques. It also means that what I have learned I have learned by making mistakes. Some small; such as missing the rails when waxing the board. Some have been more costly. Surfing happens in the deeper water. At some point it is where every surfer must head when they are ready. But how we get there is important. Some beaches have a headland or pier that can be walked along to get behind the breaking waves without having to paddle out. Which is great — it saves time and energy. But it also means that inexperienced surfers, or even experienced ones, can rush out to the deep without being fully ready for what they are getting into.

Luke 22:24-30

An Argument about Greatness

²⁴ The apostles got into an argument about which one of them was the greatest. ²⁵ So Jesus told them:
 Foreign kings order their people around, and powerful rulers call themselves everyone's friends. ²⁶ But don't be like them. The most important one of you should be like the least important, and your leader should be like a servant. ²⁷ Who do people think is the greatest, a person who is served or one who serves? Isn't it the one who is served? But I have been with you as a servant.

> [28] You have stayed with me in all my troubles. [29] So I will give you the right to rule as kings, just as my Father has given me the right to rule as a king. [30] You will eat and drink with me in my kingdom, and you will each sit on a throne to judge the twelve tribes of Israel.

Jesus' call on our lives contains a difficult truth to get our heads around; and the culture we are surrounded by does not help. The truth is we are called to something hugely powerful where we must be gentle; something that will teach, convict, and educate others where we must be humble; something that is overwhelmingly beautiful where we must be modest. The kingdom can seem contrary like that.

The disciples know they are on the cusp of something huge. Preceding this passage here has been a shift in Jesus' activity — a more singular focus as they have progressed towards Jerusalem and this week has accelerated things considerably. Suddenly they are in the city, they are interacting with the Temple elite, they are seeing the troops from Rome, they have seen Jesus clear the Temple market and teach some explosive lessons in its courts. Something is coming and as much as Jesus has tried the disciples cannot help but get swept up in the scale of what is coming.

This passage holds the verses that underpin this whole book. That we should not seek to be like foreign kings or powerful rulers but instead assume the place of the least important. The least important at any feast is the servant you do not notice. Imagine the scene Luke is offering in this short passage; Jesus wearily quells the squabble that has broken out during the meal he has longed to have with his friends. He brings silence to the room and begins to explain: "Don't seek that sort of position or power, instead. . ." and with a gesture of his hand he signals to a young servant who is quietly collecting used plates, or carrying the wine to refill glasses, ". . . be like this servant".

The foreign kings held the power; they were the *authorities* and the *professionals*. They were born and nurtured to lead their nations; they studied at the elite schools of philosophy, probably taking a place within the military for a time, they were part of networks that would shape and define the economy. And then, when they were ready they assumed their place as King and *prescribed* the course of action with what they had learnt. But, as we can see from history, they were rarely ready for their place of power. Riddled with insecurities, without a real grasp on what they had learnt and distrusting those within their networks who would seek to manipulate or usurp their power they often acted with violence and cruelty to prop up their power and feed their ego.

The powerful rulers are described differently. Theirs is not an authoritative or professional power. Instead theirs is *commercial* or *evangelical*. They work through influence; befriending and keeping those who can be helpful, working to persuade others to behave a certain way. Often highly charismatic and likeable they would amass followings and large networks of supporters. Highly entrepreneurial they would capitalize on every circumstance or relationship to further their own agenda.

Jesus gives a strong warning not to behave in either way to his disciples.

We cannot help but see parallels with the ministers we know. Those who have attended elite theological seminaries and been placed into significant leadership within the established church and those who have toiled at cultivating their own popular brand and huge following. These are, perhaps, unfair characterisations but we sense a truth in them.

Adopting the routes of either *professionalism, authority* and *prescription* or *commercialism* and *evangelicalism* can short-cut important learning and experience. We are walking down the spit of land or pier to get behind the breaking waves rather than doing the work to paddle out. Far from saying studying or creating are bad things, but they alone should not be used to position us for service. Once we arrive at the deep we find a beautiful place: Quiet, clear water, rhythmic waves passing gracefully beneath us. A wonderful place that can bring some awful consequences if you are not ready. Trying to surf here pulls on more than we may be ready for and those quiet, majestic waves can suddenly become incredibly dangerous.

In Too Deep

The beach I surfed at most in my first few years of ministry did not offer any short-cut to get behind the waves. But I remember a session where I followed some of the more experienced surfers through to the back in a particularly big swell. I was keen to see how I would cope with these larger, more powerful sets and the other surfers had shown me a channel to get back there. It was beautiful. And as I sat on my board anticipating the first ride and appreciating the place I was in I was pretty happy with myself.

And then everyone else started paddling back further. Quickly. I was not sure what this meant so I stayed put. I had been looking towards the beach and taking in the view and failed to notice an even larger set of waves than usual was ramping up behind me. The other surfers had paddled back because their experience had taught them to keep an eye on this and to move back to get out the danger zone. But I was not ready to be out here yet. The first one just about went under me, cresting a few metres on from where I was floating. That was my first indication that something was about to happen. I turned to see a large wall of water just tipping over in time to crash on me. It was a uniquely unpleasant experience. Not any real risk of injury. Not frightening. Just humbling. I was not ready for these waters yet and by short cutting my way into them I had demonstrated both arrogance and ignorance.

Perhaps we can see similarities with ourselves. We find ourselves in too deep, we move too quick to the deeper waters, and instead of acting with humility we default to arrogance. We make dangerous decisions because we adopt the posture of a *professional*, prioritising our agenda and *prescribing* that which we know because it is our *commercial* interest. We overlook other ways of knowing because we are the *authority* and we manipulate and persuade whoever we can to our point of view because we are an *evangelical*. It is a dangerous mix and one that does not prepare us to join in with God's activity well.

Certainly we are called to these deeper waters. And when we approach them with the gentleness, humility, and modesty of a servant they there is so much joy and excitement to be found. But if we rush to jump in without allowing the water to prepare us for what it offers we will likely make some painful mistakes.

The deeper waters are best visited with an experienced guide. I am self-taught in surfing but after the experience of being pancaked by an unanticipated set of larger waves I had a coffee with Matty, a friend who worked as a surf instructor, for him to give me some pointers. When we approach any ministry, service, or work as a Christian it is vital we find someone who can speak into what we are doing. Someone who can listen to us, share some experience, point out when we are not paying attention.

Practice Spiritual Direction.

Not Every Wave

THE TEMPTATION FOR NEW SURFERS, having paddled out, having reached the deep water where the waves come as beautiful rising peaks, hopefully having paused for a moment to appreciate the peace, is to launch into frantic activity trying to catch every wave. Each one is full of potential and possibility. Each one may be the one that offers that perfect ride. The trouble is that it is quickly exhausting.

Luke 5:12–16

Jesus Heals a Man

¹² Jesus came to a town where there was a man who had leprosy. When the man saw Jesus, he knelt down to the ground in front of Jesus and begged, "Lord, you have the power to make me well, if only you wanted to."
¹³ Jesus put his hand on him and said, "I want to! Now you are well." At once the man's leprosy disappeared. ¹⁴ Jesus told him, "Don't tell anyone about this, but go and show yourself to the priest. Offer a gift to the priest, just as Moses commanded, and everyone will know that you have been healed."
¹⁵ News about Jesus kept spreading. Large crowds came to listen to him teach and to be healed of their diseases. ¹⁶ But Jesus would often go to some place where he could be alone and pray.

We have had a unique insight over the past few months into the *clean* and *unclean* that we observe in Scripture. COVID-19 has opened our imaginations beyond suspecting the Pharisees and Jewish community of just having peculiar taboos thought up by legalistically minded leaders. Instead we can now grasp, in some measure, the strict isolation of those with highly infectious diseases. Yet, in Jesus' compassion he reaches out to heal that man. Not simply of his leprosy; but of the social, spiritual, economic, and emotional oppression that would have ensued from it.

Yet, he asks him not to tell anyone. He sends him to do the usual cultural rite of presenting himself to the priest and making an offering. The priest was the person who would arbitrate on matters of who must be excluded and who could be included. Jesus' actions are contrary to so much of the logic and assumptions with which we are surrounded. Jesus' desire is that the event remains secret; un-broadcast, unadvertised, not capitalized upon. And when his hopes are dashed and the large, curious, and excited crowd arrive he apparently gives them the slip.

In our imagination we think every wave should be jumped at. That when something good happens we must share it: And there are many tools to do that instantly and effectively and widely. We imagine that whenever an opportunity presents itself we must cease it. And that whenever a crowd appears we must hold onto them. Herein we show our *commercialism* and our *evangelicalism*. In honesty, I am probably not speaking from experience here — I cannot think of a time I have ever drawn a crowd in my ministry but I can remember how quick I was to tell people the numbers of our Youth Congregation when attendance hit a peak, or numbers at our Youth Project when they became large enough to feed my ego. I was capitalizing on the crowd and I can remember the anxiety it would provoke each week hoping we would have just a couple more than the week before. We see this repeated within our institutions as they produce headline statistics on social media about all they have undertaken. And the greater the scale, the greater the anxiety. It stems from the *commercial* church culture and social priorities with which most of us have been surrounded:

To capitalize on everything, despite it commodifying the people we are amongst and turning them, quite literally, into just another tally mark.

As well as commodifying the crowd, we also *commercialise* our relationships. At some point most of us will have been challenged with that favourite of; "If you only had an elevator ride to give someone the gospel, what would you say?" Answers on a postcard please. Similarly we have sat in meetings where someone has been trying to persuade us that God has offered us this opportunity and we must take it. Often that person is the church leader and they do it from the pulpit. It is tantalizingly close to spiritual abuse; invoking the will of God to convince and manipulate.

It is a result of *commercialism* and *evangelicalism* permeating our church. Every opportunity must be ceased, capitalized upon, and then commodified into a result that is broadcast for appreciation. It is the consequence of a church growth movement that sprang up with the hope of ending the rapid decline almost every denomination has experienced in the past 60 years. It has been recapitulated in many ways; some very explicit, some more subtle, and nuanced, but all with the underlying desire and motivation to save the church as we have known it.

Surfers must perpetually reposition themselves to be in the right place to catch a wave and paddling into the wave takes huge amounts of energy. To then miss it, reposition and paddle again takes a lot of effort. And so newer surfers who are frantic with activity start to get tired; they wait at the point they missed the last wave and fail to reposition. Before they know it they are back in the shallows without having properly caught a ride. So much of surfing is about being patient; waiting until you are ready for what the sea is offering and having confidence that there will be another wave. Do we really imagine that God is going to stop working in the world just because our flimsy institutions cease to be? I am not convinced that many of us think that way, but we can so easily behave as though we do.

A good surfer chooses waves with care; assessing if they are positioned correctly, gauging their own energy levels, looking to see if anyone else is already on it or better positioned for it. This requires humility. It is an arrogant surfer who believes every wave can be ridden by them. Similarly, we can often arrogantly assume we can do everything in ministry. And then we find we cannot. Exhausted, aching and frustrated we will find ourselves washed ashore without having enjoyed our session.

We will have all heard many voices telling us the importance of rest and cultivating sustainable practices in ministry. Yet I suspect most of us will need at least a few experiences of this exhaustion to really learn that lesson. But beyond that, I wonder if perhaps Jesus was doing something else in giving the crowd the slip for periods of time. His public work is still new, he has only just called his disciples. Is it possible he is maintaining his humility; not allowing himself to become dependent on the appreciation of the crowd, or sustained by the adrenaline of having a few more people each day, or motivated by how much they need him? These are easy traps to fall into and Luke helpfully reminds us that we may need a break to remind ourselves who it is we are serving; not the crowd, but the Father. If we get this wrong, we end up jumping at every wave. If we are attentive to how we are positioned and what waves are right for us then we are responding to what God is doing.

Practice Slowing.

Breaking Boards

Surfing in the shallow waters or in waters with obstacles creates many risks and opportunities to damage your board. These can be attractive places to surf, but they will ding, chip, snap or smash a board and, sometimes, the surfer as well.

Luke 14: 1-6

Jesus Heals a Sick Man

> [1] One Sabbath, Jesus was having dinner in the home of an important Pharisee, and everyone was carefully watching Jesus. [2] All of a sudden a man with swollen legs stood up in front of him. [3] Jesus turned and asked the Pharisees and the teachers of the Law of Moses, "Is it right to heal on the Sabbath?" [4] But they did not say a word.
>
> Jesus took hold of the man. Then he healed him and sent him away. [5] Afterwards, Jesus asked the people, "If your son or ox falls into a well, wouldn't you pull him out right away, even on the Sabbath?" [6] There was nothing they could say.

What has challenged me about Jesus is who he ate with. Not the sinners and tax collectors — I completely understand why he ate with them. But he also goes for dinner at the Pharisees houses. Whilst we often make the Pharisees the Gospel bogey men — they appear as if from nowhere at various points and if the Gospels were a pantomime we would all shout "Boo!" when they did. But the Pharisees were reformers. They were seeking to enact a new way of fulfilling God's call to Israel that the whole nation could participate in rather than just the Priestly elite who had become corrupt and inactive. They were seeking to broaden out the faith; to make it accessible to all and engrained within the community rather than the Temple structures. However, in their efforts for this they had become elites; morally and intellectually they gained a sense of superiority to those around them. They were the religious *professionals*; they understood what Scripture said and they understood what God wanted and so they were the hope of redeeming Israel. We all find a challenging reflection of ourselves in the Pharisees; it is why they appear so often.

As such, a healing on the Sabbath posed a significant issue for them. In their *professionalism* they had extrapolated the life-giving laws of the Torah almost to absurdity. To heal on the Sabbath was an act of work; and so despite it being an action of justice, mercy, and faithfulness they could not condone it. They had a *prescribed* set of behaviours that needed to be adhered to and Jesus' action was outside of these. To the Pharisees he behaved unprofessionally and unexpectedly but to the man who was healed he acted righteously. It left the Pharisees speechless.

Jesus was aware of all this under the surface: Perhaps spiritual insight, perhaps a keen sociological mind, perhaps a good set of ears that could hear the whispers and quiet commentary surrounding him. Whichever it was he knew why they were watching him so closely. He knew their desire to determine where Jesus was positioned, where his priorities were. Was he going to adhere to their *prescribed* orthodoxy and orthopraxy or was he another uncontrollable entity whose power and popularity they could not harness?

We are not all as gifted with insight, intelligence, or even good hearing. We often miss when we are being evaluated or sussed out. We often miss the things under the surface that we must pay attention to; pointed rocks, shallow waters and old debris lurk under the waters in some attractive surfing spots. Similarly there can be pointed priorities, shallow motivations, and the unhelpful debris of Christendom lurking beneath the surface of some attractive activities that can cause significant damage.

Within my first full-time posting there were just three schools in the town. Church leaders were keen to have a presence in all of them and a group had just started as School Chaplains at the senior school. They invited me to join them and I jumped at the opportunity. We met early in the morning once a week to pray for the school; this was a singularly awkward event from the off. And each lunch time, in different pairs, we would patrol the main corridors of the school to speak to students. I found this bizarre but went along with it, often walking around for thirty minutes saying desperate "hellos" and getting ignored.

Our prayer meetings would inevitably return to reoccurring themes. They were rarely about students or staff or education or community — instead they focussed on chaplains being "allowed to share Christ" — as though by their very presence a chaplain were not a demonstration of Christ's love and hospitality. If I am honest I didn't even fully understand the premise of the prayer. Was Christ a currency that we possessed exclusively and could distribute as we saw fit? It all seemed a bit *commercial*. Once prayers had finished then pleasantries would ensure: How was so-and-so? How was this-or-that going? Again, these conversations would take bizarre turns to reach familiar destinations each week. The same old tired Christian controversies would rear their ugly and boring heads: evolution, homosexuality . . . , I thought there were more but that was pretty much it.

All this seemed odd to me but I did not think much of it beyond the members of the Chaplaincy team being odd people. I was naïvely failing to notice these obstacles lurking beneath the surface. The individuals who were constantly bringing up these issues were looking to see how I would react; looking to suss me out and position me because they had an agenda and wanted to know where I would fit within it. They had a *prescribed* orthodoxy they wanted to impose; using our prayer meetings to make this clear. They were deeply *evangelical*; using their lunchtime patrols to try and create a tribe and grow their youth club. They were the *professional* Christians, the ones who were going to redeem the church of all this needless interpretation of Scripture and inclusion of gay people. I wish I had noticed these obstacles sooner.

Eventually it all came to ahead. A very brave student challenged one of the other chaplains that God could not truly be love if He did not love her for who she was. I was not there when it happened but I can hear the voice of the chaplain ringing in my mind. "He loves the sinner but hates the sin". Obviously the school asked us all to stop coming in pretty quickly. There was a parental complaint and the school had to do some difficult work in assuring the community that they were, in fact, protecting their children.

That surfboard, that piece of ministry, got completely smashed. In fact, despite loving schools work I did not return as a chaplain to a school for another 4 years when I moved location and joined another brand-new chaplaincy team that was completely the opposite experience.

The dangers of fixed assumptions, rigid orthodoxies and shallow understandings had caused much pain, but these were not the heart of the problem in the first school. Rather it was the posture of the members of the Chaplaincy team: they positioned themselves as the *professionals*; there to straighten out Christianity for the students and offer Christ in some *commercial* transaction. They sought to *prescribe* acceptable belief amongst the chaplains. They operated as *evangelicals* seeking to draw a crowd and capitalize on the opportunity to see young people. In many ways their beliefs about creation or human sexuality are neither here nor there; any belief can be harmful if it is used in such a *professional, commercial, prescriptive,* and *evangelical* way. We all needed a deeper understanding of what Chaplaincy meant; but perhaps if I had seen the obstacles I would have chosen to surf elsewhere rather than destroying my board.

It is worth noting that boards can be repaired. Even quite significant breaks can be dealt with by someone skilled enough. But it leaves a mark — long after we have forgotten how we dropped it in the garage or ran over it in the car park — there is a tell-tale line or patch that signifies something happened. Within our activity it leaves a weak point or vulnerability. I imagine the deputy head, who bore the brunt of the parental anger, is unlikely to engage with School Chaplaincy again because of her experience. And the student, her family and her circle of friends were unlikely to engage with Christianity again after their experiences.

I did return to the school, and in fact we began a really interesting piece of school's work engaging those at high risk of exclusion with bicycle repair as a way to rebuild confidence in learning and positive experiences of school. But there was always a bit of a scar — the church had hurt the school and so a weak point had been created. But the board was rideable once more. Trust slowly was restored and God's activity was able to be enjoyed again as we dialled in the gears, resprayed the frames and went mountain biking together in the bike project.

Practice Discernment.

Spin Cycled

Spin cycled is a term that describes one of the most unsettling things that can happen in surfing. It is a given that within a session you will end up having a spill or two [probably more]; where you misjudge something and take an early splash into the water. These are common and quickly recovered from. But being spin cycled is something different. It happens when are in the wrong place, when you are in the impact zone, and the entire force and weight of a wave crashes onto you pushing beneath the waves, rolling you around in its barrel, exerting huge pressures onto you, driving you so deep that you are entirely disorientated, panicked and wondering if you are going to make it back to the surface.

Luke 4: 22-30

[22] All the people started talking about Jesus and were amazed at the wonderful things he said. They kept on asking, "Isn't he Joseph's son?"

[23] Jesus answered:

You will certainly want to tell me this saying, "Doctor, first make yourself well." You will tell me to do the same things here in my own hometown that you heard I did in Capernaum. [24] But you can be sure that no prophets are liked by the people of their own hometown.

[25] Once during the time of Elijah there was no rain for three and a half years, and people everywhere were starving. There were many widows in Israel, [26] but Elijah

was sent only to a widow in the town of Zarephath near the city of Sidon. ²⁷ During the time of the prophet Elisha, many men in Israel had leprosy. But no one was healed, except Naaman who lived in Syria.

²⁸ When the people in the meeting place heard Jesus say this, they became so angry ²⁹ that they got up and threw him out of town. They dragged him to the edge of the cliff on which the town was built, because they wanted to throw him down from there. ³⁰ But Jesus slipped through the crowd and got away.

Luke's long and important birth narrative makes clear Jesus' identity and vocation: He is the Son of God, one of David's line and the coming King, the redeemer of Israel. Luke then shifts to John's preaching where he further illumines Jesus' identity as he announces Jesus as the coming judgement. But it is not until late in chapter four where we hear from Jesus own mouth about who he is and what he believes his vocation to be. In this famous episode we hear him read from Isaiah and claim that the jubilee, the ultimate release, is fulfilled in him. We almost always finish the episode at verse 22 with the crowd wondering at this son of Joseph.

But in doing so we misread what is truly happening. In fact, often it is unhelpfully translated so we can miss the point entirely. Where it says the people were "amazed at the wonderful things he said" it should probably say they were "startled at the grace he spoke about". It puts a different light on the whole event. Those gathered in the meeting place were not impressed with Jesus public speaking ability or captivated by his wisdom; they were affronted at what he was suggesting. The mention of Joseph is not about them marvelling at a local boy made good, it is derision: "Who is he to speak like this?"

Jesus perceives their growing offence and does little to negate it. In fact, he pretty much pours petrol on the freshly kindled flames as he reminds them of God's grace for the outsiders in the times of preceding prophets and consequently lines himself up with their tradition. In particular the mention of Naaman must have sent a ripple of incredulity around the place. Naaman was a military leader from a nation Israel considered an enemy and so by referencing him Jesus brought the question to his audience's mind of whether Jesus was going to start healing Roman soldiers.

Underneath the suspicion and disquiet the crowd feel when hearing about God's grace, Jesus, I think, is experiencing their deeper emotional responses. Jesus can sense the people's desire for Nazareth's reputation to be redeemed by being associated with a powerful Jewish leader, perhaps even a messiah. This poor city in southern Galilee has felt its share of oppression from Rome, its share of disrespect and contempt from Israel. Its people are bound to desire vindication in some way. Perhaps some folks hoped for political liberation from Rome and envisaged Jesus as some guerrilla militant who would begin the revolt. Perhaps others hoped for respect of better treatment from Israel and the Jerusalem elite and imagined Jesus could be a respectable priestly leader and win them some credibility. Perhaps others, with more humble expectations, just wanted to be touched, healed, or cared for. At the very least he should heal their sick, cure their blind or renew their crippled. They have heard about the things he did in Capernaum and probably desire he demonstrate this power for them. What is the point of having someone so powerful in spirit if you cannot use them to sort some things out?

He flatly denied them. And so they wanted to kill him.

Jesus finds himself right in the impact zone. He is at the convergence of all the desires and expectations, disappointments, and frustrations of the people he is amongst. In many ways we look back at these expectations and see them all fulfilled in Jesus' ministry but not in any way they had initially been desired. It would be tempting to think that service is simplistically responding to all that is asked of you, but here we see Jesus denying the crowd: Not because he needs rest, although that is important, or because these people lack faith. He denies them because it would not truly serve them to meet their expectations or desires, nor to find quick remedies for their hurts and insecurities.

Herein we find a force we must be wary of: the desires, hopes and expectations of others for who we will be. We can all think of one or two examples where people have found themselves in the impact zone: Wrongly positioned or unaware or unready we have seen them driven under, tossed around. Perhaps we have been there in the brief moments they have surfaced to catch their breath only to see them driven under once more by the next wave. Or perhaps it has been us. For those of us who have seen good colleagues and friends hurt like this it is not an easy thing to think about.

It gets legitimised in all sorts of unhelpful ways. Some like to characterise it as spiritual attack; waving around the thoughtless adage of "you must be doing something right". Others fail to understand the severity and claim that "we've all had tough periods in our ministries". And so often the usual things are prescribed: perhaps a weekend retreat, or maybe a course in assertiveness or conflict management, or just good old prayer. None of these are bad things but they fail to deal with the issue.

We can never manage to surf in the impact zone. We are in the wrong place. To us, each wave is threatening and terrifying. The ocean comes to feel like a relentless and punishing place. It is important to remember that those same waves may be allowing someone else to enjoy an incredible ride. I mention this not to rub it in further if you are struggling, but instead to remind us that it is not the fault of the wave. We can be quick to blame God. I am all for having full-throated discussions with him, fully articulating my feelings to him. But being spin cycled is not his doing. Similarly, I believe service entails sacrifice and self-expenditure; but it must never be harmful — that is slavery and is an entirely different thing. Rather, as any surfer will tell you, getting spin cycled happens when we allow ourselves to be positioned in the impact zone; by inattentiveness or failure to perceive what is happening or by some external force which we will discuss in a little while.

Once you are in the impact zone and getting spin cycled it is a difficult place to get out from. Just as you recover from one wave another is there to put you under once more. The sheer weight of water prevents your arms and legs from working to swim, you lose any sense of which way is up or down or where the surface might be and the pressure of the depth you find yourself pushed to makes your ears ring. Sadly, I have watched friends work this way for years, even decades within their service. They have come to see it as normal.

We need not spend much time expounding how we see our five key themes at work here as they are repeating previous patterns. By allowing others to position us we are responding with a posture of *professionalism*: that who and how we are is determined by expectations. This, in turn, can create a dynamic of *commercialism* as *we* provide what *they* are asking for. These are both underpinned by *prescription* as roles, behaviours and activities are already imagined and imposed. The *evangelical* response is to try and serve the tribe with what they desire so the tribe can be strengthened. And beneath these is *authoritarianism*; that we should be impervious to these waves as we are the expert who has been prepared and anointed for the task.

But Jesus just slips away. Within our surfing analogy he manages somehow to punch through or duck-dives the wave that is over him and go on to somewhere else. He does not stand his ground to educate the crowd about what he is going to do or give them assurances of where he will take them. He just shakes it off and goes elsewhere. Not into retreat or hiding, just on to something more life-giving. In fact, the rest of chapter four is him healing and restoring people. Jesus manages to avoid being positioned by others — something we see throughout the gospels as he gives cryptic answers and makes oblique comments. He avoids being swept up in their expectations or pushed under by their desires. Where we can so easily become suffocated by these he simply slips away to find space and joy.

Practice Breath Prayer.

Getting Back In

AFTER DAMAGING A BOARD OR being spin cycled it can be a little difficult to get back in the water. Sometimes injuries must be recovered from, but more often it is about confidence. It is about remembering what happened last time and fearing it will happen again. It is not always immediate; sometimes it is only particular conditions that prick our concerns of fears.

Luke 24:30-34

> [30] After Jesus sat down to eat, he took some bread. He blessed it and broke it. Then he gave it to them. [31] At once they knew who he was, but he disappeared. [32] They said to each other, "When he talked with us along the road and explained the Scriptures to us, didn't it warm our hearts?" [33] So they got right up and returned to Jerusalem. The two disciples found the eleven apostles and the others gathered together. [34] And they learned from the group that the Lord was really alive and had appeared to Peter.

There is a beautiful and extraordinary painting by Caravaggio of this moment that I am sure you have seen. In an entirely ordinary meal-time scene Cleopas and his friend snap with recognition; shunting chairs backwards and extending arms wide they are suddenly aware they are in the presence of the risen Jesus.

You in the Water

This gives rise to another moment of resurrection. The Greek word used for resurrection is *anastasis*. If you look at the text carefully you can see that this same word appears in verse 33; "so they *got up*". They too were resurrected; they too stepped into new life at that moment of recognition. The exclamation that Caravaggio so masterfully captures holds the complex realisations that if Jesus really was risen; not just reappearing but sitting and eating with them [notice how Jesus eats in most resurrection encounters to signify the importance of the body] then he really had upended the empire. He really was the Messiah as Rome's execution had been ineffectual. His kingdom really was near as new life was bursting into the present. And if all this was true then following his pattern was the way to join in.

What I do notice is that Jesus does not tell them to get up and go back to Jerusalem. It could seem a little as though Jesus was rounding up the stragglers by catching these two on the Emmaus road, but he does not say; "Yes, here I am. Now, get you stuff together and get back to Jerusalem". Yet they intuitively know to head back. At this point it is worth remembering that to head back to Jerusalem was to head back to a city probably still bubbling with a week of controversial and inflammatory activity which had brought Jesus and his followers into conflict with almost every power holding group. To head back was to re-enter a potentially dangerous place. Yet, it was to return to the other followers, to re-encounter Jesus, to re-join God's activity. And so they go.

We are not always as quick to return to the places where we have had bad experiences. One winter a huge swell came into my local surfing spot. I prefer surfing in winter because the beaches and waters are clearer so I have more space to be clumsy and bad at surfing without disrupting anyone else. And there are generally bigger swells in winter. But this was unusually big; in fact it was too big. One wave rushed up behind me. I had attempted to paddle into it but was nowhere near quick enough, yet I felt it bump me onwards so began to get to my feet to drop in. But this wave was fast and rather than finding myself sliding down the front of the wave (where you should be) I was stood right on the peak. As it crashed I fell the full height of the wave before it landed on top of me slamming me into the sea floor. Once I washed up on the beach I sat on the shore catching my breath and assessing if there was any more significant damage to the board or myself. It was a little while before I went back in the water. And even now I am reluctant to go into waters that look like the ones that day.

I had a similar feeling in a car park outside one of the local churches after a ministers' meeting. Being amongst this group completely sapped my energy; I sat in my car trying to catch my breath wondering about the extent of the damage of the previous two hours. We had put a date in the diary for our next meeting but I had no intention of going. I was tired of it and did not want to go back. It was not big and powerful like that wave that had crashed on me; rather it was culmination of all the bickering, point-scoring, and undermining that happened at every meeting. But it had escalated this time — resulting in some personal and cheap comments. They were by no means amongst the worst things that have been said to me, nor the most offensive. But they caught me off guard. I was used to the dysfunctionality of this group but it had gotten cruel and vindictive.

Looking back I realise that there were some unhelpful postures we had all adopted. We were all heavily invested in our *professionalism*; we were not vulnerable or honest with one another, we presented the best possible version of what was happening at our churches and gave the impression that it was all under our control. The logic followed that our *professionalism* indicated whether we were right; if our thing was going well it meant that our beliefs and practices were the correct ones, if we were victorious then our god was the strongest. These meetings had become sessions of defending our orthodoxy against others.

In fact, this had gone so far it had almost become *evangelical*. There were tribes within the group seeking to win converts, or at least bring along some additional members to demonstrate their strength. I remember arriving several times and being surprised by the presence of someone uninvited and unexpected. I realise in retrospect it was others bolstering their tribe for the conflict.

Instead of being brothers and sisters sharing good news we had allowed *commercialism* to turn us into competing entities. When our youth project grew, another church invested in new equipment and changed the night they met to the same evening to reduce our numbers. When the secondary school re-opened its doors to me another minister blocked the rest of us from going to a church-affiliated school he was governor at. The insecurity, mistrust and fear had driven these postures of *professionalism, evangelicalism* and *commercialism* causing such a toxic environment that I was wiped out by it; exhausted and not really wanting to join in anymore. And I am sure others felt the same.

I never went back. I wish I had. I wish we had had an honest conversation; allowed ourselves to be vulnerable, stopped competing with another and fearing our differences. But instead we stopped meeting, got more entrenched and just sniped at one another from afar. I am pretty ashamed of some of the things I said about the others and I am fairly sure they are embarrassed about how they treated me.

Why would I go back into that? Why head back into something that is potentially dangerous, damaging, and hurtful. Why return to something that raises so much anxiety? You do not have to. I never went back to that group and while it is a regret, I believe it was the right decision. And if there is something that has the potential to be so damaging it is probably best avoided. But we still get back in the water; we are still driven by a calling to serve or compulsion to surf: But perhaps elsewhere, or in different conditions, or more mindful of the obstacles.

And we do not get back in the same. Cleopas and his friend encountered Jesus and were resurrected. As we rest on the beach we are restored. As we sit in the car park we are healed. Christ is at work renewing and reinstating.

When I moved to my second place I contacted the other ministers — there were not many. Four of us got together for a meeting. My anxiety as I went in was pretty high but I did not approach as a professional, I felt no need to win them to my tribe and I did not sense they were my competitors. The group quickly grew as churches filled vacant positions and as God moved in our town. The group had its differences but it was a life-giving and exciting place that was bearing fruit. Because we insisted on some things right from the outset: Honesty, vulnerability, devotion to mission, formation and hospitality to views that differ from our own.

If I had gone back the same, I probably would have experienced the same. But if we can encounter Jesus, we can go back resurrected.

Practice Truth Telling

Patience

Lots of surfing is about patience. Unlike a lot of sports it is dependent on particular conditions. Surfers can wait through weeks of flat water for a swell they can surf. Even within a single session a surfer must wait; wait for the right wave, wait for their turn.

Luke 2:36-38

Anna Speaks about the Child Jesus

> [36] The prophet Anna was also there in the temple. She was the daughter of Phanuel from the tribe of Asher, and she was very old. In her youth she had been married for seven years, but her husband died. [37] And now she was eighty-four years old. Night and day she served God in the temple by praying and often going without eating.
>
> [38] At that time Anna came in and praised God. She spoke about the child Jesus to everyone who hoped for Jerusalem to be set free.

Anna waited. Anna had patience. Anna knew that there was a particular wave of God's activity coming into the world and so she patiently waited for its arrival. In her lifetime there were other pseudo-Messiahs; other revolutionaries that led militias in confronting Rome and seeking to liberate Israel. But Anna patiently waited for Jesus.

Patience

There is, however, more to notice in this tiny memory in Luke's narrative of Jesus' birth. Anna's waiting is not passive. She is active in her patience. We can often think that waiting means doing nothing. When we look at surfers sat on their boards out the back of the waves it can seem as though they are not doing an awful lot. But they are not passive. They are vigilant to the waves that are coming — assessing each one, noticing each one. They are also constantly checking where they are positioned in relation to the break. We will talk about currents and rip tides shortly but the ocean is never static and your position in the water is something you must always be aware of.

Anna spends "night and day" in the Temple. This is where she waits, praying and fasting in hope. A philosopher named Cornel West said this:

> "Optimism and hope are different. Optimism tends to be based on the notion that there is evidence out there to believe things will get better. Optimism is rational and deeply secular whereas hope looks at the evidence and says 'it does not look good at all'. But hope creates new possibilities based on visions that become contagious and allow people to engage in heroic actions always against the odds."

Only a deep faithfulness can sustain patience and hope like Anna's: Only a sincere trust that God is going to do something. I have seen surfers paddle out, wait for a good wave, and give up because they have not had the patience that day. I have scanned surf forecasts waiting to see the four-to-six-foot swells I look for and seen nothing for weeks and lost hope. In our activity we can wait for waves, long for good conditions and often we are quite impatient. Anna's prayer and fasting are analogous to the surfer's attention to the coming waves and their position to them. She engages in these disciplines to maintain her faithfulness; to give her clarity of vision to perceive the true Messiah, to give her hunger to sustain her desire to see God's activity in the world.

But there is still more to this passage that Luke assumes we know but that most of us may not. Luke includes a bit of Anna's history; she is descended from the tribe of Asher. For most of us that will mean little as our knowledge of Israel's history is not that forensic. But the mention of Asher would have prompted a memory in Luke's audience. Israel started as a confederation of tribes but in their desire to be "like the other nations"[1] they asked for a King [we know this bit]. Against God's desire he appointed Kings over them; and as he had promised they were less than ideal. King Rehoboam was the last straw and the northern tribes left the nation. However, they soon found themselves conquered by the Assyrians and taken into exile long before the rest of Israel. The effect of this was so great Asher was known as one of the lost tribes; either because there were not enough survivors to be described as a tribe afterwards or because they had been in exile so long they had lost their distinctive identity.

Luke mentions this to make us aware that Anna has lived for much longer under the oppression of an empire; it is in her family history. She, more than anyone, would be longing for revolution and yearning for liberation. And yet she waits; for 84 years. She is patient and has hope that God will move. She is not swept up by the pseudo-Messiahs but waits for Jesus. And when she finds him — the one who would bring true liberation and release — she tells everyone else who was hoping with her. Her only mistake is underestimating the magnitude of God's activity; that she thinks Jesus will bring release for Jerusalem but it will be for all creation.

Most of surfing is waiting. Allowing the ocean to present what it is offering. Try to force surfing to happen makes for an unpleasant session. A surfer will end up chasing every wave, they will become exhausted from constantly paddling to where they think they might catch a ride and all they will get is short and powerless rides. We can recognise the similarities in trying to force God's activity.

We can try to make things happen by *professionalism* or *commercialism*: If we can take control strongly enough, if we can invest enough time and energy maybe we can force God, or people, to behave as we desire. Troublingly there is leadership training I

---

1. 1 Samuel 8

have witnessed, and books I have skimmed that seek to equip us with skills to accomplish this. And if we look around our church we can see the signs of where we have been fairly successful at it. Projects and programs that bare little of God's activity but through sheer determination and force of character have come to be. It is almost admirable what has been achieved tangentially to God's will. But Anna is not lured by the pseudo-Messiahs. She waits for an authentic wave of God's activity. Sensitively, and with spiritual disciplines to sharpen her perceptions, she looks to the ocean and patiently waits for what it will present.

We can also overlook that Anna responds to a baby. Anyone waiting for a Messiah would be waiting for a powerful leader; a person of power and stature. Because we are so familiar with Christmas story we easily presume that everyone was expecting the baby Jesus. But realistically no-one would be looking at an infant and saying; "He is the one". It just would not make sense. Anna does not follow the *prescription* for a Messiah and so this is how she avoids being swept up by the others. If we look for and respond simply to the things we expect then we are likely to miss a whole load of God's activity.

In recent years I have had to start talking about the God who pulls my trousers down. I should explain this. There have been several occasions where I have declared something with certainty and confidence and almost immediately God has thoroughly embarrassed me by doing the opposite. For example, in a bit of teaching on being apostles I had stated that people were never going to simply arrive at our church out of curiosity. I was trying to encourage our community to be more intentional in demonstrating faith in their lives rather than just randomly inviting people to church services. I was desperately trying to move us away from the church growth mentality of: Faith happens in our building on a Sunday so people should come and join in with it. The next Sunday a lady arrived and said, "I'm not sure why I'm here really, I think God sent me" — she has been a much-loved member of our community ever since. The God who pulls my trousers down. We must seek to be attentive and sensitive to what God is doing rather than *prescribing* what we think he should do.

Anna may be a prophet but she is *non-authoritative*. Luke makes this clear by describing her as an old woman; a childless widow from a forgotten tribe. Luke is not undermining her by drawing our attention to this; quite the opposite. Luke's is a highly egalitarian gospel when read carefully; he so often positions the women as the faithful, responsive, and courageous characters against the incredulous, slow-minded, and cowardly male figures. Perhaps it would be good for us to remember that the church has always been sustained by the hope of old women — even before it was birthed. I think Luke mentions Anna's situation deliberately; after all he could have just said "Anna, a prophet" and not lost much from the main narrative. But we have these details so we recognise that against all the noise of the *authoritative* were the uncredentialed voices. Where the Pharisees, teachers and leaders do not recognise Jesus, the shepherds, the old women and the demon-possessed Gentiles do. Perhaps it is because they must have more hope and less optimism or expectations about what they are waiting for.

Practice Fixed-Hour Prayer

Good Honest rides

Eventually, after paddling out, after waiting, after careful positioning, after being attentive to what the ocean is doing you catch a ride. And something incredible happens: A moment of transcendent beauty, a connection between ocean, board, and rider. It is electrifying and peaceful, exhilarating and calming. If you surf it is difficult to describe to others, and if you do not surf it is the thing that surfers will try and describe to you. I have reached the conclusion that it is better just to say it was a good honest ride.

Luke 6:43–45

A Tree and Its Fruit

> [43] A good tree cannot produce bad fruit, and a bad tree cannot produce good fruit. [44] You can tell what a tree is like by the fruit it produces. You cannot pick figs or grapes from thornbushes. [45] Good people do good things because of the good in their hearts. Bad people do bad things because of the evil in their hearts. Your words show what is in your heart.

We intuitively know when we have been in the presence of goodness; when we have heard, seen or tasted the goodness Jesus is speaking about here. We feel blessed by it, enriched by it. Often we want to share what we have witnessed with others. And often we find our language falls short. When we describe that goodness it can sound too simple, too humble. But we experience it nonetheless, foretastes of the coming kingdom, moments of the future rushing into the present. These are instances that are both hugely exciting and deeply peaceful.

Our language is important. As Luke points out, the way we speak indicates what is at the core of our being, and so we must be attentive to our language. It is troubling how much we have adopted our lexicon and parlance from what John might refer to as "the world". I am reluctant to use this phrase as it can create a dynamic of dualism; instead we might refer to it as the empire[1] which I think is a helpful, but complex term. Even so, much of how we speak, and therefore how we imagine and operate, is grafted onto us from the *professional, commercial,* corporate, and institutional paradigms with which we are surrounded. Within our activity we may use phrases like business models, project proposals, expansion schemes, plans, results, development goals, programmes, etc. These probably do not contain bad intentions; in fact they are probably desires for hopeful, kingdom centred ministry. But because we have been profoundly shaped by our culture we approach the fulfilment of these earnest intentions with the only means we can imagine: We try to appropriate the activity of the empire into the life of our church. And the two simply do not mix. It is like looking for strawberries on a stinging nettle.

In an essay on education called "The Iron cage revisited" scholars Paul DiMaggio and Walter Powell first used the phrase "institutional isomorphism"[2] which I have found helpful in describing this subtle process of changing to be like what we are surrounded by. We notice it personally when we are amongst a group and begin to speak a bit like them. And we notice it institutionally as we see the denominations we are part of shaped, or misshaped, by adopting practices and priorities and policies from elsewhere. This said, I have a strong belief that God can use all things for good, but we must be attentive to what we are giving space to in our

---

1. It would be worth reading David Benjamin Blowers 'Kingdom vs Empire or Walter Brueggemann's 'God Neighbour Empire'.
2. DiMaggio & Powell *The Iron Cage Revisited* 147

heart. I was in one meeting within my denomination discussing a new venture. The proponents were emphasising how important it was to move quickly to capitalize on our "commercial advantage over the others";what they meant by this was that we needed to move quickly before *other churches* began to do the same. Since when could churches be *other*? I lost interest at this point. What we say belies our priorities; and the priority here was making a name, catching a headline, or "cornering a market".

Jesus' example of the good and bad trees is slightly convoluted. Why would you be trying to pick figs or grapes from thorn bushes — thorn bushes are pretty obviously not fig trees or grape vines. I suspect it is because we are not good at distinguishing good from bad. They sound antithetical and yet can look almost identical save for the flavour of their fruit. Those ministers or examples we know of who seem to "make things happen" tend to be two categories: Those who are singularly gifted in using the world's tools; manipulation, politics, marketing, and branding to build their empires. You can hear the way they operate in how they speak. These people are often celebrated, yet they are never fulfilled. The ride was never good enough, the wave was never big enough. Often, when they leave for the next thing whoever follows finds, behind the façade and the headline stories, a world of pain and manipulation.

The other category is who are ultra-sensitive to the Spirit and work at positioning themselves to be responsive to what God is doing. They speak differently from the first group; they have not made complicated and grand development plans; instead they tell compelling stories about what they have seen God doing. They do not generate schemes and programmes but seem to find these natural patterns or events they can bless and be blessed by. When we find someone like this they are worth listening to. And when you peer into what they do behind the scenes you will find people enthused, equipped, and empowered to serve.

Surfers all know when someone is exaggerating; embellishing their story to give it more grandeur or excitement. We can smell it. What they say gives away their insecurities about their abilities and their dissatisfaction with the session in the water — they wanted it to be greater, grander, more noteworthy. Similarly, we all love to hear someone tell us about a good, honest ride. No embellishment, no ego — just someone sharing something they really enjoyed; that transcendent moment of connectivity. It is exactly the same in ministry. We know when someone seeking to impress us with attendance numbers to an event or embellishing the story of what actually happened. And we know, we can sense, when someone is sharing something good. Good trees mean good fruit.

Servanthood then, is *non-commercial*. It does not adopt the practices of success that is sees in the world, seeking to replicate the empire's strength even if it is with good intention. Those serving must maintain postures of *non-professionalism* and of being *non-authoritative* so that they can be positioned attentively rather than forcing their own way. This entails *non-prescriptive* activity; responding to the subtle shifts and gifts of God which contradicts the short-and long-term planning of the corporate paradigms we can become so familiar with. It is *non-evangelical* in that it does not seek to persuade or force others to join with our agenda but holds participation loosely.

Practice Celebration.

Discipline & Practice

It could sound like surfing is an effortless activity. That trying to force it, or chase every wave, or work hard is not being advocated. This is not the case. Surfing takes practice and discipline. You must be in the water, you must work on your paddling out, on your skill and connection to the board, on your dropping in. Repeating and refining all these is essential for enjoying surfing. The beautiful reality is that if you enjoy surfing; if you are doing it because you are compelled to, then the practice and repetition is no hardship because you are doing what you love. Those motivated by wanting to call themselves surfers, or just wanting a few pictures for their Instagram of being stood up on a board are unlikely to be up at dawn enduring the rain and the cold ocean — because it is not what they love.

Luke 12: 32-34

Treasures in Heaven

> [32] My little group of disciples, don't be afraid! Your Father wants to give you the kingdom. [33] Sell what you have and give the money to the poor. Make yourselves moneybags that never wear out. Make sure your treasure is safe in heaven, where thieves cannot steal it and moths cannot destroy it. [34] Your heart will always be where your treasure is.

It may be a little harsh, but the church is a pretty anxious place. Maybe not everywhere or in all things but there is a palpable anxiety. Perhaps it has always been there but I suspect that it has been steadily rising since the collapse of Christendom. We were simply not ready for our empire to fall. This anxiety can lead to grasping and accumulation. Grasping for significance and power; for a platform to stand on and feel secure. Accumulation to create stockpiles; to build storehouses in case the provision runs out. Yet, Jesus assures his "little ones" that their Father wants to give them the kingdom. A kingdom which is abundant so that accumulation is not necessary and a kingdom that is affirming so that grasping is no longer required. And then he utters a beautiful phrase to hear that is incredibly difficult to fully understand: "Your heart will always be where your treasure is".

It has become one of those verses that is beautifully calligraphied and printed and sold to be put up in people's homes so that it is understood that their home and family is that which they most treasure. It is wonderfully negligent that Jesus has just instructed his followers to sell their homes. But this is not why I mention it. I mention it to talk about disciplines and practice.

Heart, within the Biblical cultures, did not signify the same sentimental centre of affection that it has come to represent in our culture. Heart was the centre of a person; the seat of the intellect and will, energies and devotions. We touch on devotion lightly, perhaps, with our understanding of heart, but this is far more robust. Jesus was saying something about how his disciples would orient their entire beings and lives. Jesus is saying you will shape your life around what you prioritise. This rings true for us individually, for our churches and for the church. For example, a person or church who is primarily concerned with orthodoxy — right knowing — will devote much time to studying the Bible and reading the work of theologians. Those who have great hearts for compassion will give much energy to working to bring healing and comfort to those in distress. Those who seek power and position will apply themselves to getting noticed and achieving status.

Discipline & Practice

There are many helpful books about spiritual disciplines; but the reality is if you do not have the desire to do them, you will not sustain them. You may manage a fast or two so that you can tell other people you fast. You may go on a retreat for a weekend's rest. But ultimately, where your heart lies will be determined by what you desire most. Most of us seek enjoyment and a feeling of wholeness, but when we cannot get these we settle for being either entertained or distracted. Enjoyment and wholeness take time and effort, energy, and perseverance.

Surfers practice paddling into a wave and dropping in endlessly. The better one can get at this, the more likely one is to catch those really special waves that enable the most exciting rides. I am a terrible swimmer — in fact I cannot really swim much at all. But I have had to work and work on my paddling to make sure I can get out in the bigger swells. In the same way, as servants we must routinely be conditioning ourselves to serve well, be positioning ourselves attentively and be practicing actions so that we can catch on to, and truly enjoy, God's activity.

If approached as a route to feeling superior, or simply as tasks that must be accomplished, the spiritual disciplines will feel dry, boring, and unnecessary. But, if approached because they are where the heart is; because there is a desire and hope to be a servant and so there is a need to be conditioned, positioned and practiced then the disciplines can feel freeing, life-giving, and vital. It is not hardship to practice because you are just practicing the things you love.

Surfing quickly became part of my regiment of spiritual disciplines. It is where I am in silence; there is not much point speaking with no one else around and I have not found a way to have headphones in the water yet. It is where I am in solitude; I am a fairly anti-social surfer and usually go on my own. It is where I can contemplate, pray, and listen as well as so much more. This regular board meeting has, at times, been the backbone to my spiritual formation when everything else has been neglected. Surfing really has been my salvation in some ways.

Servanthood requires conditioning, positioning and practice which arrive by the disciplines. But they also serve the purpose of decentralising the ego; we are not the centre of our world, and so can help strip away our pretentions and preferences for *professionalism* and remove our sense of being *authoritative*. Having said that, there is a risk of becoming proud of our spiritual disciplines and using them to feed our ego. We may instrumentalise them to prop up our *professionalism* or our being *authoritative*. The disciplines are intended to indicate the abundant generosity of God who is present to us, attentive to us, mindful of us in ways we cannot reciprocate and so the disciplines function *non-commercially*. When approached *commercially* they become very dangerous activities as we engage in them believing they are earning us something or crediting us in some way. Whilst they may, by their nature, seem *prescriptive* they are actually the means of releasing us from the *prescriptions* of the world to be busy, hurried, productive etc. When we use the disciplines themselves as prescriptions; when we suggest prayer or retreat as a solution to a problematic situation, then we often hollow them out.

Practice Rule for Life.

Energy

SURFING TAKES ENERGY, WHICH IS finite and must be replenished. Surfing without energy is recipe for disaster and can create some dangerous situations. Whilst energising and exciting there is no denying that it depletes the surfer and cannot be indefinitely sustained. But energy is never lost; Newton taught us that. It can only ever be transferred.

Luke 9: 10–17

Jesus Feeds Five Thousand

[10] The apostles came back and told Jesus everything they had done. He then took them with him to the village of Bethsaida, where they could be alone. [11] But a lot of people found out about this and followed him. Jesus welcomed them. He spoke to them about God's kingdom and healed everyone who was sick.

[12] Late in the afternoon the twelve apostles came to Jesus and said, "Send the crowd to the villages and farms around here. They need to find a place to stay and something to eat. There is nothing in this place. It is like a desert!"

[13] Jesus answered, "You give them something to eat."

But they replied, "We have only five small loaves of bread and two fish. If we are going to feed all these people, we will have to go and buy food." ¹⁴ There were about five thousand men in the crowd.

Jesus said to his disciples, "Have the people sit in groups of fifty." ¹⁵ They did this, and all the people sat down. ¹⁶ Jesus took the five loaves and the two fish. He looked up toward heaven and blessed the food. Then he broke the bread and fish and handed them to his disciples to give to the people.

¹⁷ Everyone ate all they wanted. What was left over filled twelve baskets.

I am not sure why it is, but I have rarely preached on or based any teaching on this passage. There are key stories in Scripture that often remain Sunday School favourites and are rarely re-explored in the more mature stages of faith. And yet these passages are vital, compelling, and deeply interesting. This one is certainly more than Jesus the friendly magician cooking up lunch for everyone, which is how I had understood it for a troubling long time.

Often my starting point for a passage is to look at what is contained in the Bible footnotes and I enjoyed what I found so much I want to share it even though it adds nothing to what we are about to talk about. In verse 13, where the disciples describe the provisions they have, there is a little star by "small loaves of bread" that leads you to a note at the bottom which says "these would have been flat and round or in the shape of a bun". Perhaps I am missing something significant in this, in which case I apologise, but it seems as though whoever added that footnote believes I have never seen a bread roll before or lack the adequate imagination to understand what could be meant by a small loaf of bread.

Anyway, amusement at footnotes aside, this passage chimes again with an ancient story which Luke uses to shape his readers understanding of what is happening. Out in the desert bread is miraculously provided. It is a recapitulation of a key moment in the Exodus story. Luke uses this shorthand to announce his story is going to be about a journey that leads towards liberation and the establishment of a new humanity. By the end of this chapter in Luke's gospel the journey towards Jerusalem and the cross and resurrection has begun for Jesus and his disciples.

Energy

Having dusted off this story and given it some proper consideration I have come to believe it is about more than a supernatural picnic. I think it is a story about generosity. What I am about to say may sound like I am denying a miracle but I am acknowledging one that seems to articulate a greater truth than this being a demonstration of Jesus' catering capabilities: That as the disciples shared what they had with generosity it changed the hearts of a people to be similarly generous with what they had. The danger of privatising property, provisions and power is that some go hungry. The miracle of holy redistribution is that everyone can eat all they want. After all, if we believe the miracle is that Jesus saw hungry people and so employed his sovereignty and divinity to feed them it raises some problematic questions for us. Principally, why does he not still extend that ability to feed hungry people?

Instead, if we read the text within the context of Luke's broader narrative about Jesus' message and vocation then it becomes a miracle of transforming 5000 people's hearts to be outward looking, not to privatise provisions but to be generous. This seems to fit with the rest of Luke's work; most obviously episodes such as Zacchaeus, parables like Lazarus and the Rich Man, and the famous passages in Acts 2 and 4 which describe common possession amongst the followers of Jesus.

But what is useful for us is the reality that Jesus had been taking the apostles for a retreat at the time. They had just returned from being dispatched to the villages to tell the good news and heal and Jesus' intention is clearly that they should be alone. Yet, a crowd follows them and Jesus teaches and heals until late in the afternoon. Everything is indicating that energies are spent: Physically, emotionally, spiritually, economically. Yet Jesus is able to redistribute; to transfer energies. Where the disciples thought they had hardly anything left to give Jesus pointed out that theirs was not the only source of supply.

We can find ourselves responding as the disciples when tasked with feeding the crowd: we simply do not have enough. This positions us *authoritatively* or with *professionalism*: It can only be our resources or energy that is drawn upon. When we are willing to be humble and receive from those we are amongst we may find an unexpected abundance. When I was working as a Youth Pastor I started by preaching every week; I thought it was my duty, my responsibility, as the leader to feed my people. After all, that is what I had always seen modelled. But as the months went on I got more and more tired. This was not my full-time job; at the time I was teaching at secondary school and fitting in about 20 hours of work for the church a week. A young man, a key part of the worship team, asked if he could preach. I would love to say I said yes straight away but I did not. Eventually, though, we arranged a Sunday where he would give the teaching. It was one of the best sermons on putting on the armour of God I have ever heard. And it inspired others who came forward to teach over the next few months. We were well fed because we shared what we each had with generosity.

Similarly, we must be careful about privatising our energy; adopting a posture of *non-evangelicalism* will mean that we do not only give our energies to that which benefits our tribe. When I arrived in my first full-time post I offered the local churches that if they ever needed any help with anything I would be happy to be there. No-one responded. I suspect they were fearful that I was going to "sheep rustle" members of their congregation as they knew mine was declining rapidly. However, once I closed our Sunday gathering, so had nowhere to take any rustled sheep, slowly the invitations began to come. And slowly some barriers began to be removed between churches. I was not privatising my energy but transferring it.

Within Luke's account energy is not spent but transferred — as the disciples give so others give. I think that is a miracle. In Luke Johnson's "The Literary Function of Possessions in Luke-Acts" he concludes that within Luke's writing "possessions are a sign of power"[1] and so when the disciples share the power they have they realise that within the crowd they have far more than they could have hoped for; an abundance. When we give our energy in service it is not spent — this is quite an ego-centred view of what is

---

1. Johnson *The Literary Function of Possessions in Luke-Acts* 221

happening reducing it to a *commercial* transaction. Instead, energy is simply transferred. Power becomes shared, universalised. And so at our sites of service more begins to happen.

When we are surfing well we are drawing on the energy of the wave as much as possible. When we first learn to paddle into a wave we start furiously paddling way too soon. As we improve our technique we reduce the amount of energy we must put in by becoming more sensitive to the wave and using its energy. We cannot generate enough energy alone to move the board quickly enough to stand up; surfing can only happen in relation to a wave. In the same way service works best when we are joining in with God's activity and others' power. Those things we try and do using our own resources and energy will quickly exhaust us. The more sensitive we can be to what He is doing the more we can transfer energy. Because there is an abundance: There are no shortage of waves and we do not use up their energy by surfing them. There will always be more than we can gather.

Whilst I have not paid enough attention to this story in the past we do regularly retell it within Christian worship. It can be so commonplace that we may miss the extraordinary and subversive and revolutionary aspects of the Eucharist. For me this ceremony embodies four huge ideas: 1) *Abundance without avarice.* There will always be enough to go around. We do not have to be concerned about whether we are at the front or back we will receive what is needed in contradiction to a world that perpetuates a narrative of scarcity and competition for resources. 2) *Power without hierarchy.* Regardless of any status or position everyone gets the same and nothing is held back from anyone. 3) *Vulnerability without fear.* We kneel and put ourselves into a position of submission and yet we need have no anxiety. We acknowledge our need without nervousness. 4) *Gentleness without weakness.* The Eucharist is a subversive act. It is a sign that we are not dependent upon that which the world would want us to be and yet is so peacefully and gently administered.

Practice Holy Communion.

CURRENTS & RIPS

A COUPLE OF THINGS THAT surfers must be aware of are the currents and potential rip rides in the waters they surf. A current is a fairly constant flow within the body of water in a particular direction. These are large and easy to spot although are still dangerous. Rips however are more tricky: They are powerful channels of water at the surface that drag surfers out away from the beach. The instinctive reaction is to swim directly against them but this can exhaust quickly and is sadly ineffective.

LUKE 4: 1-13

Jesus and the Devil

¹ When Jesus returned from the Jordan River, the power of the Holy Spirit was with him, and the Spirit led him into the desert. ² For forty days Jesus was tested by the devil, and during that time he went without eating. When it was all over, he was hungry.

³ The devil said to Jesus, "If you are God's Son, tell this stone to turn into bread."

⁴ Jesus answered, "The Scriptures say, 'No one can live only on food.'"

⁵ Then the devil led Jesus up to a high place and quickly showed him all the nations on earth. ⁶ The devil said, "I will give all this power and glory to you. It has

been given to me, and I can give it to anyone I want to. ⁷ Just worship me, and you can have it all."
⁸ Jesus answered, "The Scriptures say:
'Worship the Lord your God
and serve only him!'"
⁹ Finally, the devil took Jesus to Jerusalem and had him stand on top of the temple. The devil said, "If you are God's Son, jump off. ¹⁰⁻¹¹ The Scriptures say:
'God will tell his angels
to take care of you.
They will catch you
in their arms,
and you will not hurt
your feet on the stones.'"
¹² Jesus answered, "The Scriptures also say, 'Don't try to test the Lord your God!'"
¹³ After the devil had finished testing Jesus in every way possible, he left him for a while.

In my foundation year of fine art studies, before starting my BA, my tutor asked me a question that had a profound impact on my painting practice. Until that point I had followed current trends or painters I admired; I was in my immaturity so was shaped by whatever was new or interesting to me. He asked me very directly "What kind of painter do you want to be?" Until that point I had never considered this. I had the capacity to make choices about how I worked in the studio, how I operated, how I used materials etc that would have huge effects on the end results. It took a couple of years for me to get close to having an answer although I am still not sure I do. But I do know the best painters are ones who have got to grips with it and found the painter they wanted to be.

I feel as though this passage is Jesus answering the question; "What kind of Messiah do you want to be?" I have come to think it is a story about much more than Jesus resisting temptation by knowing his Bible inside out. Jesus is defining his vocation, perhaps for himself, but more likely Luke is using this to illuminate his readers. He resists temptations that would undermine that vocation; temptations to prioritise providing for himself, to corrupt his faithfulness in return for power and to become insecure about his identity and safety. The re-telling of Exodus is once again apparent as God provides sustenance, security, and the affirmation of identity.

The implicit call for us to similarly resist these temptations to provision for self, to power and to protection is certainly a challenging one, yet one we have seen repeated in Luke's gospel: Those seeking to create a safety net for themselves are turned away from following Jesus, those with the means to make significant provision are similarly rejected and those looking to save their life are warned they will lose it.

Jesus could have chosen to be a conquering military Messiah, such as Simon Bar Kokhba who successfully liberated Jerusalem from the Roman Empire a century and a half after Jesus. Similarly he could have chosen to be a priestly Messiah such as Judas Maccabaeus who had expelled the Seleucid Empire a century and a half before Jesus and re-established Temple worship in Jerusalem. There are parallels in their vocation and yet Jesus' activity is profoundly different. His understanding of what it meant to be the Messiah was entirely alternate.

Those within any sort of ministry are surrounded by currents or rips at any given time. Either slow but definite drifts in a particular direction or powerful unexpected rips that tear outwards. These flows are not always bad. For example, in the wake of George Floyd's murder in May 2020 there was a powerful rip; a surge of imagination towards social justice. This forceful flow dragged some churches into considering some issues that had gone unaddressed for too long; it took them back to the deeper waters so that they could reflect and repent. Skilled surfers often use currents or flows to get to where they need to be in the water. Similarly, Jesus was not averse to using power. In fact the previous section sees Jesus provide in a miraculous way. But it is about positioning. If a flow can take us to where we need to be then that is helpful; if we have the skill and experience and self-awareness to navigate this then it can be of benefit. But when a flow drags us to somewhere we should not be or positions us unhelpfully then obviously we are in trouble. Similarly if we do not have the skill or experience to realise when this is happening it can be a frightening experience.

It takes a skilled and observant surfer to really recognise what is happening in the waters. There are micro and macro movements that can indicate powerful forces. I suspect most of us notice them; we sense them, feel them around us. We may even have momentary reactions. But we are a long way from understanding them; naming and describing them and considering what they may be doing to us; even further from establishing a coherent response.

To list or explore what these rips and currents might be within our ministry contexts is probably too great a task for a section or even a single book. And were we to begin to name them undoubtedly there would be some that appear incredibly dangerous to some that others were happy to utilise to position themselves. There would be some that were seen as harmless and inconsequential that to others would be alarming and cause for grave concern. As it is with the waters so it is with our situations.

Surfers must determine their own movements to properly position themselves. They may use flows and currents but with great caution. Determining our own movements is not to assert our individualism or suggest that we become the masters of our fate but it is to suggest that we are mindful of the influences upon us; that we name and describe them; that we recognise where they would take us and we make decisions about whether that is where we should go. This self-awareness is crucial in service to ensure we are in the place where we can be of use. We can easily succumb to a *commercial* mentality where we can provide more and more of what is desired but this may lead us to subservience or being instrumentalised. Soon we start neglecting that which is important for the sake of that which is popular. Similarly the defined routes of *prescription* can promise to lead to where we want to go but can quickly drag us to an undesirable place.

Some years ago a colleague of mine invested a lot of time in learning the prescribed techniques for Church Planting. By her own admission she knew the process inside out; each required step or stage was clear in her mind. The church appointed her to a newly built community and she set about implementing what she had learnt. Soon she found herself managing a building and providing activities and programmes; she had formed a young and vibrant congregation and was nurturing a leadership team. Her denomination saw a wonderful success. However, managing the building and all the activities was meaning she could rarely attend the programs she had started and was meeting fewer and fewer of the community she lived amongst. The congregation all drove into the estate for Sunday's as they were Christians who had left other churches in preference of her style and the novelty of this new plant. And the leadership team were not making decisions based on serving the community they were within but on what would benefit the Sunday gathering most. She had followed the *prescription* to the letter and found herself far from where she had hoped to be.

There was quite a distinctive building at my local surf spot; easily spotted from the water as it was quite ugly in its own way. It would serve as my indication of when I was being carried off by the current. It is not that I had to stay close to the building. But it enabled me to know where I was by my relation to it. We must value these anchoring points, even if they can appear less than desirable at times; they may be people we know, or traditions and practices we observe but they can be valuable points of reference that allow us to explore further than we might otherwise.

Currents and Rips are particularly dangerous when we are tired. In Luke's account the Tempter appears at the end of Jesus time in the desert; when he is hungry, when presumably he is at his most tired. The temptations may be a constant presence in our realities but it is only when we are tired we become attentive to them. When they begin to exert any pressure or force upon us if we are lacking energy we can do little to resist them. At times they can even feel like they are making up for our tiredness; lending us a power and direction that we had lost. This danger makes knowing when to stop essential; knowing when we need a moments rest or even when our session is over but we will talk about this soon.

Practice Liturgical Prayer.

Enjoyment

SURFING IS ENJOYABLE. IT CAN be hard, it can be frustrating, it can be dangerous but it is centred on joy. It is centred on experiencing something profound; being connected with the energy of the ocean in a unique way.

LUKE 9: 28-32

The True Glory of Jesus

> [28] About eight days later Jesus took Peter, John, and James with him and went up on a mountain to pray. [29] While he was praying, his face changed, and his clothes became shining white. [30] Suddenly Moses and Elijah were there speaking with him. [31] They appeared in heavenly glory and talked about all that Jesus' death[a] in Jerusalem would mean.
> [32] Peter and the other two disciples had been sound asleep. All at once they woke up and saw how glorious Jesus was. They also saw the two men who were with him.

They saw the true glory of Jesus. His beauty, his power, his truth. It is worth looking at the section of Scripture in its entirety and realising that this transcendent moment is followed by a failure of the disciples to heal a boy and by Jesus speaking about his death. Jesus' glory was not just about illation and euphoria; it is about restoring some pretty ugly situations that will be painful to face and it is about submitting to the worst the world could offer to upend the empire. Without all of this in the picture any enjoyment will feel like pretty hollow hedonism.

Nonetheless, the disciples have an incredible, mountain top experience. They enjoy it so much they want to remain there; like surfers staying on a wave too long.

In surfing, the ocean is offering you a transcendent experience; a moment where you will be in synchronicity with the energy of the ocean, when you will be enabled to dance and carve down the line. When every sense will be enlivened by what is happening around, within and through you. In service, God is offering us this same experience: moments of synchronicity with the will and intention of the Creator, when we are empowered to see his true glory revealed. When every sense is enlivened by what is happening around, and in and through us. If you're not enjoying it, you're not doing it right.

Practice Gratitude.

Finishing a Ride

GETTING OFF A WAVE AT the right time is something we all must learn. It seems counter-intuitive to new surfers. They have managed to finally get to their feet, they have managed to remain upright, why wouldn't you stay there as long as possible? But the wave washes out and eventually you are in the shallows, trickling along looking a bit silly.

Luke 9: 33-36

> Moses and Elijah were about to leave, when Peter said to Jesus, "Master, it is good for us to be here! Let us make three shelters, one for you, one for Moses, and one for Elijah." But Peter did not know what he was talking about.
> [34] While Peter was still speaking, a shadow from a cloud passed over them, and they were frightened as the cloud covered them. [35] From the cloud a voice spoke, "This is my chosen Son. Listen to what he says!"
> [36] After the voice had spoken, Peter, John, and James saw only Jesus. For some time they kept quiet and did not say anything about what they had seen.

The figure of Peter within the Gospels is a gift for a teacher; so often he gives voice to what we may have been given to thinking or assuming. Oddly this has made him a figure of fun or criticism within some preaching; Oh Peter! You never understand. And yet if we are honest so often we would have responded in the same way. Perhaps that is why we are so quick to highlight his immaturity; it is often the bits of ourselves we recognise in others that we criticise most harshly in them.

Once again in this episode Peter voices what we all would think. It reminds me of the party game or ice-breaker favourite; "if you could have dinner with anyone from history...". Of course Peter would choose Moses, Elijah, and Jesus. They are the greats from his tradition, the leaders of his people. Of course he wants to stay. Of course he recognises it is good for them to be there. But we are reminded, less than gently, that this desire to remain is not the ultimate intention. Nonetheless, for Peter this was the transcendent moment; he has followed Jesus, learned from him, leant heavily into this new way of living and finally he is wrapped up in the activity of God, standing amongst those who have gone before. This is Peter's ultimate ride.

But that is not all service is about. As we have said, there is much more to surfing than just standing up.

I have the tendency to milk a wave for more than it has to give. I have mentioned I am not a strong swimmer and by the time I have paddled out to the break and managed to paddle into a wave I have expended a lot of effort and energy and I want to get the most out of a wave before I relinquish it. Sadly this often means I find myself drifting to a slow halt and finding myself in the shallows with a long paddle back to where I need to be. In fact it is probably costing me far more energy to surf this way and yet it is a habit that is difficult to break.

Similarly it can be very hard for us to know when something needs to stop. We inherit project or programmes that are well established, that may even appear healthy and fruitful, but have been drifting for a while but no one wants to call it. When surfers get towards the end of a wave, or there is little energy in one, you will often see them pumping the board; pushing it into the wave trying to re-find some energy or momentum. We can sometimes approach these established programmes in this way; if we can just inject some energy, re-find some momentum in it. Probably there

Finishing a Ride

is little harm in this, but I wonder what wave we may be missing as we try to sustain one that is finished. Additionally, I wonder how difficult the subsequent paddle back is going to be because we have allowed ourselves to get so far from the break.

I am also not very good at choosing my waves. In a set you may have 5 or 6 waves of which 2 or 3 may be good rides. Often these are towards the end of the set but frequently I am not patient enough to wait. And so I must put in a huge amount of energy to get the board moving quickly enough to catch these lesser waves. If I manage it I am reluctant to give it up.

At my first full-time position there was little programme in place — most things had closed or were on the brink of closing and so it was a bit of a blank canvas. The building was in a beautiful location on a popular street and so I thought a Community Café Space would be a good idea. We could foster community, support the vulnerable, build relationships, provide engagement for elderly residents who were finding the town increasingly isolating; it seemed that there were so many positives. So I sought grants, purchased equipment, spent ages designing a cool logo. It never really worked. A few people frequented the building — we did an exercise class for older people for a little while, we got a brilliant kitchen volunteer, and some relationships were made. I liked that I was available for a few hours just to be with people. But there were also days when it was just me and a couple of volunteers. But I had put so much energy into it, and I was so pleased with the logo, that I did not have the courage to call it and get off that wave. I just let it drift along until my last year when I realised I was going to have to pass this on unless I did something. That bit of the program closed and it made room for some far more interesting things.

I think some of the fear of getting off a wave is that there may not be another one: That this was *the* one for us. Certainly early in our ministry this is a nagging thought — that if we do not make it work then that will be it. I guess the longer we are in the water the more we come to realise there really is a lot of waves happening. But perhaps we fear for our ability to catch another; but if we can be sensitive to what is happening and ensure we are positioning ourselves well then this need not be an anxiety. And if we do paddle into the wrong wave it is acceptable to withdraw our commitment to it. It is not a failure. Herein we catch a glimpse of *non-professionalism*: We do not have to make things work or make things permanent. Similarly it is *non-commercial* as there is no need to extract absolutely every possibility from every wave. And nothing is wasted. In a future venture that logo may return and my long conversations with that kitchen volunteer when no-one else was there gave me some beautiful insights to Buddhism.

Like Peter we must celebrate and wonder at the transcendent moments, aware they will end but knowing that there will be more along the way.

Practice Rest.

Finishing your Session

At some point our session must end. We cannot remain in the water for ever. Bodies fatigue and rest beckons from the shore. This can be difficult. Sometimes, as the sun is setting and the waves are particularly generous we can just want to remain in the beauty catching ride after ride. However, sometimes we feel like we have not really caught anything and are reluctant to leave the water as we do not feel we have not really done what we came to do. In either situation, knowing when to get out can be hard.

Luke 2:22-35.

Simeon Praises the Lord

[22] The time came for Mary and Joseph to do what the Law of Moses says a mother is supposed to do after her baby is born.
They took Jesus to the temple in Jerusalem and presented him to the Lord, [23] just as the Law of the Lord says, "Each first-born baby boy belongs to the Lord." [24] The Law of the Lord also says that parents have to offer a sacrifice, giving at least a pair of doves or two young pigeons. So that is what Mary and Joseph did.
[25] At this time a man named Simeon was living in Jerusalem. Simeon was a good man. He loved God and was waiting for God to save the people of Israel. God's

Spirit came to him [26] and told him that he would not die until he had seen Christ the Lord.

[27] When Mary and Joseph brought Jesus to the temple to do what the Law of Moses says should be done for a new baby, the Spirit told Simeon to go into the temple. [28] Simeon took the baby Jesus in his arms and praised God,

> [29] "Lord, I am your servant,
> and now I can die in peace,
> because you have kept
> your promise to me.
> [30] With my own eyes I have seen
> what you have done
> to save your people,
> [31] and foreign nations
> will also see this.
> [32] Your mighty power is a light
> for all nations,
> and it will bring honor
> to your people Israel."

[33] Jesus' parents were surprised at what Simeon had said. [34] Then he blessed them and told Mary, "This child of yours will cause many people in Israel to fall and others to stand. The child will be like a warning sign. Many people will reject him, [35] and you, Mary, will suffer as though you had been stabbed by a dagger. But all this will show what people are really thinking."

I should pre-empt any concern that I am about to draw an analogy between finishing a surf session and dying. I am not. But Simeon serves as an interesting figure to talk about rest, peace, and fulfilment. He and Anna are two old people that Luke concludes his birth narrative with; by means of reminding his readers of that this story began long before the birth of Jesus. Matthew achieves this with a genealogy and John with a re-framing of creation so we can see almost all the gospel writers are keen to draw our imaginations backwards.

Luke's description of Simeon is, like Anna's, quite deliberate. A "good" or "righteous" man announces a little chime in our minds;

Finishing your Session

a remembering of someone else. Job. I think we are intended to make this connection with Job, a man who is without comfort and peace in his life; a representative of an Israel that was trying to understand why so much tragedy had befallen it. The parable of Job is an early, yet sophisticated, exploration of theodicy. To be reminded of him is to be reminded of Israel's long, peace-less, difficult history that it was yearning to be delivered from.

And Simeon is satisfied; he can die in peace — meaning he can live in peace. He has seen the fulfilment of the Lord's promise to deliver. Interestingly, he sees it at the commencement, not at the fulfilment. Simeon needs nothing more to perceive God's activity other than to see the infant Jesus. He never hears him teach or sees him heal; he does not see the tables turned or the loaves redistributed: Just the infant Jesus. He sees the start of God's move to bring peace and that is enough. He can get out the water satisfied.

It is not always as easy for us to know when we are done: When we are finished for the day; when we need to rest at the end of a week; when it is time for a holiday; when a project or programme is concluded; when it is time for us to move to a new placement; or even when we are finished with full-time ministry. The temptation is always to just do a bit more. One more wave.

Sometimes this is because we are really enjoying it. The conditions are just right; low sun, perfect wave size arriving in neat, well-spaced sets, clear water. We get a few sessions like this and we want to spin them out. But we cannot stop our bodies getting tired. Whilst we are energised we are expending energy. And no matter how efficiently we surf this will always be the case. But the temptation is to stay for one last set; one final ride. Many surfers will tell you that this is invariably when a session is spoilt: The ride that dings a board, the unpleasant wipe-out that taints the beauty of the session, the jelly-fish sting to the foot that makes the walk home a painful ordeal. These are all risks that are present during the whole session and yet somehow they only seem to happen just after you should have got out.

It is often the same in ministry. If only we had not opened that late email. If only we had not picked up that call. If only we had not popped our head in to see how things were going. We must know when we are done for the day; because when we are tired we can spoil a whole day's work; damage a ministry by saying something ill-thought-through, make a poor decision that tumbles us about, get stung by a comment we should not have read or heard until we were feeling refreshed to cope with it. They can happen at any point in the day but they always seem to happen just after you should have gone home.

These repeat and even escalate as the time-scale increases. A (much older) friend of mine who was nearing retirement was at a beautiful church. His wife had become ill with a growth on the brain. His congregation responded wonderfully and compassionately but her behaviour began to change and it was hard for them to remember this was the result of the growth. He had been meant to leave in the April but the new minister could not begin until the September and so he agreed to stay in post for a few extra months. Things had been going well for several years and a few months seemed manageable. His wife's condition was nowhere near life-threatening, just a mild inconvenience. Except the decision to stay seemed to up her aggression. And the distinction between this anger and the result of the growth became hazy at best. Within a few short weeks from his decision she had said some pretty hurtful things to various members of his church. But these were easily forgiven. The problem came with him defending her comments and reinforcing the hurt. He was understandably tired; exhausted. But these events spoilt a good session right at its end, after he should have got out.

Wear a watch. Set a time that you will get out no matter what.

We should resist the urge to keep going; to accomplish more or to be more productive. After all, we have gone to a lot of effort. Surfers have spent time getting to the ocean, getting the wetsuit on, preparing the board — they want to make the most of being in the water. But they must know when they are finished. It is a demonstration of *non-commercialism* — they do not have to extract every last drop. It is better to have 10 amazing rides and leave well than finish with 2 terrible ones and leave frustrated. Similarly

Finishing your Session

we have gone to a lot of effort: daily prayer, equipping others, our minister's training, fundraising for projects, moving ourselves and perhaps our families to new places. It can pressure us to ensure we get the most out of it and often our response to that pressure is to try and do more: To extend our working day, to just glace at the inbox before bed, or just return that call. Similarly our week can stretch when we allow events to fill our day off in the diary. Our sessions can stretch and stretch increasing our risk of being so tired something tragic, stupid, or harmful happens.

I am encouraged and challenged by Simeon. To have the faith to find peace at the commencement rather than at the fulfilment is quite something. The term "finishing well" is often used and this could be understood to mean tying up all the loose ends; finishing all the projects, making sure everything can be picked up and continued. But I have come to see that perhaps finishing well is leaving when we see it is right to leave regardless of how things stand. We so often long to see the fruit of our labours; the end of a project of the fulfilment of an idea but surfing teaches us that waves are endless. They do not stop when our session finishes. It is not about what we are doing but what God is doing. And when this truth gets into our heart our choice to rest; to finish for the day, the week, the season, or session, becomes so much easier. We can trust God to do what he is going to do rather than believing we must see it all through.

Practice Sabbath.

Others in the Water

"That's my Wave" & Cutting in

Someone who is new to the ocean, unsure of the waves and equipped with a hard, pointy, fast-moving object can be a bad combination. This has made many surfers quite territorial. There is a strict etiquette in surfing. When you join a line up [surfers waiting at the back of the water to catch waves] you cannot just go for the first wave you see. There is protocol; others who have priority. As more and more people take to the water and line ups get bigger and bigger this is becoming quite a point of tension as people get possessive over waves and others get impatient with waiting for their turn. Cutting in, which is when you drop in on a wave in front of someone already on it thus cutting off their ride, can be the end result and is both inconsiderate and dangerous.

Luke 7:36-50

Simon the Pharisee

A Pharisee invited Jesus to have dinner with him. So Jesus went to the Pharisee's home and got ready to eat.
[37] When a sinful woman in that town found out that Jesus was there, she bought an expensive bottle of perfume. [38] Then she came and stood behind Jesus. She cried and started washing his feet with her tears and drying them with her hair. The woman kissed his feet and poured the perfume on them.

³⁹ The Pharisee who had invited Jesus saw this and said to himself, "If this man really were a prophet, he would know what kind of woman is touching him! He would know that she is a sinner."

⁴⁰ Jesus said to the Pharisee, "Simon, I have something to say to you."

"Teacher, what is it?" Simon replied.

⁴¹ Jesus told him, "Two people were in debt to a moneylender. One of them owed him five hundred silver coins, and the other owed him fifty. ⁴² Since neither of them could pay him back, the moneylender said that they didn't have to pay him anything. Which one of them will like him more?"

⁴³ Simon answered, "I suppose it would be the one who had owed more and didn't have to pay it back."

"You are right," Jesus said.

⁴⁴ He turned toward the woman and said to Simon, "Have you noticed this woman? When I came into your home, you didn't give me any water so I could wash my feet. But she has washed my feet with her tears and dried them with her hair. ⁴⁵ You didn't greet me with a kiss, but from the time I came in, she has not stopped kissing my feet. ⁴⁶ You didn't even pour olive oil on my head, but she has poured expensive perfume on my feet. ⁴⁷ So I tell you that all her sins are forgiven, and that is why she has shown great love. But anyone who has been forgiven for only a little will show only a little love."

⁴⁸ Then Jesus said to the woman, "Your sins are forgiven."

⁴⁹ Some other guests started saying to one another, "Who is this who dares to forgive sins?"

⁵⁰ But Jesus told the woman, "Because of your faith, you are now saved. May God give you peace!"

Luke's construction of this narrative scene is quite brilliant. The three figures are positioned carefully: Simon, the affluent and self-righteous Pharisee is hosting this event. Meals were not the intimate gatherings of friends that we would recognise; more like public events that centred on a political or philosophical debate. [more Question Time than Come Dine with Me.] Jesus is in the

"That's my Wave" & Cutting in

middle of all this: the controversial and increasingly popular Rabbi who is there to be at the centre of this debate. And then the woman; the uninvited guest whose behaviour is undignified and inappropriate. We probably recognise the caricatures that Luke is sketching.

Simon, who seems to have an openness towards Jesus, or at least enough curiosity to listen to him, is probably wanting to explore the depths of Jesus' Scriptural knowledge, hear his insights into their socio-political situation, engage in a discussion where he can probe Jesus' intellect and probably demonstrate his own. We have all met people like that. I remember being invited to a fellow minister's house for a meal and him growing increasingly frustrated as I talked to his children about their experiences at school more than listening to him tell me about the weighty tomes of theology he had been reading. We see a similar frustration rising in Simon as the woman draws the attention from the glittering conversation he should have been hosting to a scandalous and embarrassing scene.

He wants to cut off what she is doing, draw the evening back to what it was supposed to be about. After all, she is just a lowly nobody. We do not even learn her name. She is not qualified to enter into this event; she can observe like the others, listen in from the doorway and perhaps be edified by the experience. But she certainly should not be taking to the stage. Like a more experienced surfer selfishly cutting in on a learner's wave Simon assumes priority because of his position, because he perceives parity with Jesus, because he is the *authoritative* host and *professional* voice.

Until Jesus makes the observation that she is doing what he had neglected. She has positioned herself as the servant within the scene; washing Jesus' feet, greeting him, and anointing him. Luke positions her as the faithful one despite how undignified and inappropriate her behaviour is; despite how unprofessionally she behaves and how unauthoritative her position.

There is a surfing etiquette that is vital to grasp. If someone is on a wave before you do not cut them off. If there is space great. But if you will cut them off you let it go — even if it is a great wave, even if you are in a great spot for it. Even if you think you are a better surfer than them. The truth is you do not know what you will prevent by cutting them off. It is your ego that claims priority over them. "I've worked harder for it" or "I'll do it better" or the old narrative of scarcity: "There won't be another wave".

Our *commercial* imaginations can lead us to similar postures if unaddressed. We are *professional* Christians; we have worked hard to get to the position we are in; focussing on our disciplines, responding to his call, and so can believe are deserving of Jesus attention or respect over others. That somehow we have earned something by all that. And so we can become outraged when his priority is elsewhere: Like when a surfer sees some newbie on a foam learner's board catching an amazing wave. But throughout the Gospels[1], in particular Luke, we find Jesus trying to make it clear that we will find his grace outrageous and unacceptable. We need not look much further than the elder brother in the Parable of the Two Sons. No matter how much we may profess to be ok with it, no matter who we are, at some point God's grace will be too wide for us; too inclusive, too radical.

There is, however, an important balance to be struck here. New surfers who are unaware of the etiquette and unsure of the waters can be at best a frustration and at worst simply dangerous. There will always be places to hire a board and have a go without any experience or coaching. And getting people in the water is generally a good thing; I really do not want to sound like a grumpy surfer put out by crowded beaches — there is more than enough space for everyone in the water. But great consideration is required. Before you drop in on a wave you need to have checked the situation pretty thoroughly.

A few years ago I was met a guy who was struggling with an addiction. He had reached the point where he had enough of chasing highs and we began to talk about the recovery process. I am no expert in this so was linking him with practitioners and specialists [please note there is no problem with genuine professional people in case what I am saying about being *non-professional* is

---

1. Matthew 20: 1–16 is a great example.

confused]. Most weeks he would come and see me for a coffee and let me know how things were going. Occasionally he would not turn up but often he was there, albeit late. However, one week he was fairly on time and very excited. He had met some people who could cure him. My heart sank. I know little about recovery but I know enough to know there are generally no cures — just hard yards of work on self. These miracle workers were Christians he had met at an event who were going to deliver him from his addiction. Ministries and boards are similar and have served as a good analogy throughout my explorations of learning to serve. And both ministries and boards can be incredibly dangerous if used improperly. Richard was not cured. He just became hurt and disillusioned. And we stopped meeting because I was, in his mind, a Christian like them.

Negotiating waters that are filled with people can be tricky. It requires consideration, awareness, and cooperation. I generally surf alone but one of my best surfing experiences was a perfect summers evening; the waters were cool and clear; the swell was four to six foot on an incoming tide with just a slight offshore breeze. Anyone with a board was in the water. And it was beautiful. People whooped and cheered good rides. Children were encouraged and helped along. Friendships were made and an overwhelming sense of gratitude was palpable as we sat and marvelled at the experience we were having. I mention this to balance up the other points. Having lots of people in the water can lead to some beautiful things. When we transfer this to ministry I believe the same applies.

Practice Community.

SUPs & Bodyboards

THERE ARE MORE THAN JUST surfers in the water. Bodyboards have been around for a while and is probably how most surfers began. And more recently Stand-Up Paddleboards [SUPs] have grown to be hugely popular. The response of surfers is varied. Some are pleased to see others enjoying the water. Others fear their space and primacy is being threatened.

LUKE 9: 49-50

For or against Jesus

> [49] John said, "Master, we saw a man using your name to force demons out of people. But we told him to stop, because he isn't one of us."
> [50] "Don't stop him!" Jesus said. "Anyone who isn't against you is for you."

With such a short except there is little to say but the main point; which centres on Jesus' rebuke of the disciples' tribalism. We can only imagine how these couple of lines of Luke's gospel rang out to those early Jewish followers of Jesus struggling to accept the new Gentile inclusions into their lives. We need not spend time exhausting the parallels for Christians in more recent years.

When we peer behind what the disciples say we see their motivations; they are Jesus' chosen disciples, they are his students and the ones who will inherit his Kingdom. Once again their desire for position and power lurks beneath the surface. And perhaps a narrative of scarcity; their anxiety being if these new groups start springing up here-and-there of people declaring Jesus as Lord then it will draw focus from them; that there may be diversity in belief and practice. Jesus does not seem concerned about this: "Whoever isn't against you is for you". This phrase is picked up intact from Mark's original gospel whereas Matthew uses an inverted version of the same phrase that we probably recognise more; "Whoever is not for me is against me". Both Mark's and Luke's read with greater inclusion, the category of inclusion rests just on a lack of opposition. (This is not to say Matthew is not inclusive, he works harder in his gospel to emphasise Jesus' inclusion of the Gentiles than the other writers — he just uses Mark's phrase in a very different episode).

Surfers can be uneasy about sharing the water. SUPs and Kayaks are able to get out behind the breaking waves to where surfers line up. They are a different thing entirely. You can surf on a paddleboard or a kayak but it is different; it looks different, requires a different set of skills, it has a slightly different language. Body boarders tend to be in the shallower waters riding waves that surfers have finished with. And yet all are enjoying the activity of the ocean, joining in with its energy and beauty. From within our tribes, Christians can be very suspicious of others; uneasy when they engage in activities we have quite imperialistically decided are our own. We criticise their different approaches rather than celebrating them. This tribalism may arise from our *evangelicalism*; that desire to make others just like ourselves or understanding that what they are doing now will, in time, lead them to become like us. I had always understood body boarding as practicing for surfing but more and more I meet people who do it out of preference. Similarly, I had assumed paddle boarding was for surfers whose knees had gone until I got my own and discovered what an entirely different experience it is.

When we look at this short episode in its context within Luke's gospel we can see that Luke is doing something quite clever. Just a few verses before, in the episode where Jesus heals a boy

Others in the Water

with a demon[1], the disciples were unable to force the demon out and Jesus, in verse 41, has some harsh words to say to them about this. Perhaps this is what instigates the argument that ensures at verse 46 about who is the greatest — as the three that witnessed the transfiguration have returned from the mountain with Jesus, an event that is already perhaps feeding their ego, they find the rest have failed to accomplish what is by now a common exercise within their ministry. Jesus' response to their argument is to advocate humility. But the contrast of the disciples failing to force a demon out and the report of these *others* achieving it in Jesus' name is noticeable. Perhaps Luke is warning his audience about creating factions or tribes within their communities; or in relation to other groups of followers of Jesus that were appearing around the area. Perhaps it is intended to mitigate any feelings of primacy amongst older churches or more established communities.

Once we are open to sharing the waters, not clinging to feelings of primacy or priority, then we can enjoy and celebrate the activity of others in the water; even those who are a long way out of our tradition or experience. We will probably learn something from them.

Practice Hospitality.

---

1. Luke 9: 37-43

Conclusion

No exploration of Jesus would be complete without considering the climax of his ministry; the point to which his vocation led him. I say this mindful that for many the cross has been over-emphasised; treated as the only purpose Jesus' life served or the only real piece of his ministry that matters to us today. I would firmly reject any reduction of Jesus to a sacrifice or the impact of his life to an appeasement but these are well-trodden arguments that are more than adequately dealt with elsewhere. Nonetheless, if servanthood is seeking to be centred on the person of Jesus the cross must be given consideration and I believe it to be the ultimate revelation of the postures of servanthood that I have used throughout this book.

It would be easy to misunderstand what I am saying here as this statement is only a hair's breadth from something I do not believe. I do not think that Jesus is simply serving us atonement on the cross; working as our substitute in some transaction of absolution: Firstly, because I am not convinced by the doctrine of original sin. Secondly, because I am not compelled by the traditional theories of atonement. And thirdly, because this reductionist understanding simply does not seem to fit with the texts that describe Good Friday or how Jesus himself is reported to have spoken about it his crucifixion. That said, there is little space within this book to explore what I do understand the images of Easter to mean in any detail. Instead I would like to briefly re-visit our five postures and observe how they are present at the cross.

The cross is *non-professional*.

It is apparent that Jesus is not the Messiah that anyone anticipated. From Simeon and Anna through to Judas, Jesus does not meet the criteria or expectations of the Messiah. The cross does not look like a revolution; there is no driving the gentile oppressors from Israel's land to once again establish the rule of YHWH and restore the Temple. Rome is not ejected and Herod is not dethroned. The cross looks like the antithesis of this; Rome is the victor and Herod retains his position.

In this way to cross appears highly *non-professional*. Jesus does not meet the expected criteria; he does not behave in the proper manner; he does not solve Israel's crisis or perform the anticipated tasks of a Messiah. A professional brings their power and resources to bear on a situation to achieve a desired outcome. The path to the cross, right from the crib, is one of Jesus laying down his power, forgoing the available resources to achieve something that no-one around him wanted. Even the Pharisees had warned him of Herod's desire to kill him, his disciples had been uncomfortable, even angry at his repeating that he would be killed. And yet Jesus pursues this course to the cross.

The cross is *non-commercial*.

Too often the cross is read as a transaction; that his death buys our forgiveness, rectifying this overly simplified reading has been accomplished admirably elsewhere. Instead we think about how it is *non-commercial* in the sense that it is a rejection of the profit or profile, power or position that is sought by commercial activities. Jesus was stripped — the little he had was taken from him. He was mocked — the crowd jeered and the soldier's teased about how the cross signified all his claims were seemingly untrue. He was beaten and bound — physically he was so bereft of strength that he could not carry the crossbeam symbolising how bereft of any power he had become. He was executed as a lowly criminal — there was no sense of grandeur or distinction that sometimes our images of the

Conclusion

crucifixion create for us; this was a run-of-the-mill, business of usual execution of a common criminal for the empire.

The cross is *non-prescriptive*.

If there were a manual on liberating oppressed people written pre-Jesus it would not say "Allow the oppressor to execute you". Leading liberation from oppression was about insurrection; about gathering militia, about taking back from the oppressors, about naming yourself as the rightful king, about declaring the oppressors' guilt to justify your violence and to sweep others up into it. But Jesus stands this on its head.

Rather than gathering a crowd or militia to himself, everyone fleas from him, apart from the women. Instead of denying or resisting the oppressor, Jesus says to give to Caesar what is his and to turn the other cheek. Instead of naming himself as King he does not make any claim to political power in front of Pilate. Instead of pointing out the guilt of the oppressor he asks for forgiveness for the people. In every way then, Jesus confounds the prescription for liberation.

The cross is non-evangelical.

Were Jesus' intentions to establish a tribe there are many things within his ministry he would have done entirely differently. The cross is a glaring example of this. Jesus invited those that would follow him to "take up their cross". This is not an invitation that could be taken seriously. Not an invitation that would be welcomed. *Evangelicalism* has had to work hard to twist the cross into something that is seen as a benefit to individuals; something that can be offered to them to gratefully receive. But it has come to seem at odds with what Jesus was doing. Rather than gathering a crowd to himself, on the cross Jesus scatters his followers momentarily. Rather than establishing his position as King the cross seems to deny Jesus' rule.

The cross is non-authoritative.

The path to the cross was the ultimate submission. Jesus yielded to the physical power of the soldiers, to the religious power of the teachers of the law, to the political power of Pilate, to the cultural power of Herod and to the social power of the crowd. In no way is he portrayed by Luke as adopting an authoritative position en route to the cross.

Jesus also seems unconcerned about what these groups believe about God through what he is doing: He does not educate the teachers or Pilate about the subtext of what is happening. He merely submits to fulfilling God's will through submitting to their power. And yet the criminal realises what is happening. "Remember me when you come into your power". I take this as an encouragement — The leaders, the crowds, the elite may not see the power of servanthood, but those at the very edge of the margins; those who are being crucified by the empire, can see the new reality that is ushered in by Jesus' servanthood. Perhaps the same might be true for ours.

Bibliography

Blowers, David. *Kingdom vs Empire.* Phoenix: Smashwords, 2013.
Brueggemann, Walter. *Praying the Psalms: Engaging Scripture and the Life of the Spirit.* Eugene, OR: Cascade, 2007.
Brueggemann, Walter. *God, Neighbor, Empire: The Excess of Divine Fidelity and the Command of Common Good.* Waco: Baylor University Press, 2016.
Calhoune, Adele. *Spiritual Disciplines Handbook: Practices that Transform Us.* Downers Grove: InterVarsity, 2005.
Di Maggio, P. J., and W. W. Powell. "The Iron Cage Revisited: Institutional Isomorphism and Collective Rationality in Organizational Fields." *American Sociological Review* 48.2 (1983) 147–60.
Gramsci, Antonio. *Selections from the Prison Notebooks of Antonio Gramsci.* London: Lawrence & Wishart, 1971.
Hays, Richard B. *Echoes of Scripture in the Gospels.* Waco. Baylor University Press, 2016.
Johnson, Luke. *The Literary Function of Possessions in Luke-Acts.* Missoula: Scholars, 1977.
Marx, Karl. *The German Ideology.* Amhurst: Prometheus, 1988.
Shaia, Alexandra. *The Hidden Message of the Gospels: Four Questions, Four Paths, One Journey.* New York: HarperCollins, 2010.
Tickle, Phyllis. *The Great Emergence: How Christianity is Changing and Why.* Grand Rapids: Baker, 2008.
Wells, Samuel. *The Nazareth Manifesto: Being With God.* Chichester: Wiley Blackwell, 2015.
Wright, N. T. *Paul: A Biography.* London: SPCK, 2018.

www.ingramcontent.com/pod-product-compliance
Lightning Source LLC
Chambersburg PA
CBHW050821160426
43192CB00010B/1851